THERE IS AN ELITE GROUP,
WITH A LIMITED MEMBERSHIP,
CALLED

THE SUPERRICH

DO YOU KNOW HOW THEY GOT STARTED ON THE ROAD TO WEALTH?

AND WHEN THEY HAD ACHIEVED THEIR HUGE DOLLAR STOCKPILES, HOW THEY SPENT THEM?

Martin Ackerman—that flamboyant media tycoon—and his beautiful wife Diane, can answer those questions. The Ackermans can show you how to live as if you were rich even if you aren't. They will tell you how you can control your money, even in the face of skyrocketing inflation. They will tell you how you can make money even while you spend it on luxury items and travel. The ideas presented here by the Ackermans could change your attitudes toward your investment funds, your bank accounts, your spending priorities—and your life.

LIVING RICH

BY MARTIN AND DIANE ACKERMAN

PLAYBOY
PAPERBACKS

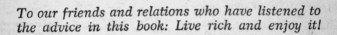

To our friends and relations who have listened to the advice in this book: Live rich and enjoy it!

ACKNOWLEDGMENTS

People often ask us what we do to earn a living. It seems that that is the first question everyone asks when meeting a new person. When we answer that we are learning to live, they seem more perplexed than ever. But, in truth, that is what we have been doing these last three years: learning to sort out our lives so that they are more meaningful to us.

This learning process is partially revealed in this book, and for the contents of the book, we have to thank the many people who have been frank with us in discussing how they live and whether they have realized what they expected from their lives. In the end, especially with fellow Americans, they usually got around to the subject of *money*, and whether that single goal of most Americans is really as important as it's cracked up to be. We'll let you come to your own conclusions.

The next book is always a little easier than the one before, but without Gay Search, Roz Cole, Cathy Hommel, Mickie Mackay, Mike Cohn, Lillian and Herman Meckler, Fernande Chiesa, Kelly Ackerman, Debra Ackerman, Vicky Ackerman, and Richard Ackerman, there probably would not have been a next one.

CONTENTS

1

INTRODUCTION

Just because this book is about rich people, don't think that it doesn't apply to you and your way of life. You may well be asking yourself how you can live rich when you earn so little money or have so little to spend or invest. If that's the case, then this book should teach you one cardinal rule: It's not the amount of money you have that counts, it's how you spend and invest what you have. Learning from the rich is the best way to become rich.

According to the U.S. Bureau of Census, 76 percent of the U.S. population, or approximately 41,919,000 families, have an income of $5,000 to $25,000 per year. In addition, there are 5,112,-000 families (9 percent of the population) earning $25,000 per year or more. If you earn somewhere between $15,000 to $25,000 a year, chances are that you have probably been able to save some money over the years, say perhaps $15,000. How you invest that $15,000 may make the critical difference in how you are going to live in the future because there are two sides to the "living rich formula." The first is income—what you earn, and how you can increase those earnings. The second, and the one this book is about, is learning how to manage what you have more effectively. It's a very simple idea: If you spend less money but spend it more effectively, then you require less money to live well.

Living rich is a concept we developed from our own experiences. It is based on understanding how to use what you have more effectively. It requires you to manage your money better, to re-think how best to spend, save, and increase the money you earn on investments by learning how to do it effectively. With such an understanding and reorganization, almost anyone can live rich.

The idea for this book originated on a quiet Sunday afternoon in London. I was relaxing after a lovely luncheon my wife had cooked and served for ourselves and four guests. It was a perfect lunch—quiche Lorraine, served with chilled Gewürtztraminer wine by Beyer, salad of water-cress and endive, a platter of cheeses with crusty French bread, fresh fruit salad and homemade apricot cakes followed by espresso. Later, puffing contentedly on a Davidoff number two cigar, I retired to my study to peruse the figures prepared for my 1977 tax return. Leaning back in my tilt-ing desk chair, I nearly fell on the floor as I broke into a cold sweat and was heard to shout, "My God, where has all my money gone?"

A little here, a little there and, in the end, a total that was staggering. Thoughts ran quickly through my mind. Yes, we live well, but not ex-travagantly; many of our friends seem to spend much more money than we spend. Yet, in the cold light of that afternoon, the numbers at the bottom of the profit-and-loss statement were mind-bog-gling—and depressing.

According to all we have read, we were rich. Anyone with a household income above $50,000 a year is rich, and in the United States there are only 500,000 similarly blessed families. Clearly something was very wrong. We were in the "rich" category, but our tax return said we were poor and indicated, furthermore, that at the rate we were spending we'd be getting a lot poorer in the future.

Your initial reaction may well be, "Having trouble keeping his spending under fifty thousand dollars a year? I should have such problems!" But just ignore all those zeroes for a moment and think back to your first job. Can you honestly say that today, several years and several pay raises later, you have fewer financial problems than you had then?

Everything is relative. You may well be earning five times as much as you were ten years ago, but because of inflation and your more discriminating tastes, the home you now live in, the clothes you wear, the car you drive, the food you eat probably costs five times what they did then! Not to mention taxes. We can honestly say that we know very few people who have more than enough money to support their life-style once they have paid their taxes.

Obviously then, *making* more money is not necessarily the answer to your problems.

The desire and drive to make money is a natural and honest one and it is possible today for anyone with moderate intelligence who is willing to learn and anxious to expand his horizons to become rich. Incredibly, the Internal Revenue Service estimates that within the next few years America will have acquired the staggering total of 371,000 millionaires. In our last book, *Money, Ego, Power—A Manual for Would-Be Wheeler-Dealers*, we tried to tell the story, as candidly as possible, of at least one way to make a lot of money—by becoming a "wheeler-dealer." We took the reader step by step up the ladder of success, and by "success" we meant success as measured by the earning of money: money for a better lifestyle, money for freedom, and money to make more money. We outlined a plan of action from getting your foot on the first rung, through education, motivations, the friends you should make and the people you should influence. We tried to give an insight into gaining experience in the right job, in the right company, choosing your line of attack and carrying through your first deal to the top.

The message of that book, and one that can bear endless repetition, is that there is nothing wrong with making money. Hell, it's the most fascinating game in town, and every bit as exciting in its own way as spending it, which is what *this* book is all about.

But making money, while exciting, is not easy, and keeping it once you've made it is even harder. I remember one of my first clients, an early 1960s wheeler-dealer, J. Arthur Warner, telling me, "Marty, if you think it's hard to make, wait until you see how hard it is to keep what you have made."

He was right. It seems that no matter where you turn today it's costing you money. Money for personal possessions, the everyday living expenses, housing, cars, travel, clothing, children and so on. Then there are the investments to contemplate, some good and some bad, all theoretically designed to give you a hedge against inflation and earn you a little more money to spend, so that you don't have to dip into your capital.

Believe me, it's harder not to spend it than it seemed at the time to make it. But if it's any consolation to you, the predicament is by no means exclusively yours. Holding onto the money is a problem that affects almost everyone, rich or not, as you will see from the chapters that follow. The Super-Rich may have more houses, their own airplanes, whole holiday resorts, while you only have one house in the country but they have to pay taxes and meet bills, too. So do the inherited rich, although they usually have a larger pool of capital to dip into when—and it is "when," not "if"— ends don't meet.

The only groups that have found any solution to the problem are those that can live off their corporations—the large, public ones—or the owners of small but very profitable companies. Their solution? Taking on the U.S. government as a 50-percent partner in their spending, if not in their profits. For every dollar spent on "living rich," the government contributes fifty cents. Simple, but very effective. And don't think that because the Securities and Exchange Commission and the Internal Revenue Service have announced an investigation into the extent to which corporate executives are using their company funds or equipment for personal gain, it will make much of a difference. Living off the American corporation is a way of life and the system is not likely to change, in practical terms, for a long time.

Taxation presents no problem for those who live rich at no cost, since they have no money, only style, talent and charm which enable them to live rich courtesy of those who do have money. You might adapt the idea using style, not money, to make money, or you could try living rich at half the cost, like some of our friends. Of course, no matter what you do, you must keep up appearances, like some of those we talk about in the chapters that follow.

But regardless of where your money comes from, what you do with it in terms of investment is the key to living rich. Indeed the investment of your capital and any capital that you can borrow and use for investment may be the true test of whether you will have anything to spend at all. Fortunes have been dissipated by poor investments made under the so-called prudent-man rule. Wealthy people, totally unprepared for earning a living, have been forced out into the work force because of poor money management. Whether you have $25,000 or $25 million to put away, if you don't understand the proper way to invest, there is little chance that you will ever have the opportunity to "live rich." More important, you may find that your life's work has been for naught. With today's rate of inflation, even to stay as poor as you are now you need to understand the power of investment.

What this book can teach you is how to invest for fun and profit—where is the best place to put your cash; the ins and outs of savings banks, certificates of deposit, Eurodollar bonds, the stock market, art and other financial matters; how to stay out of commodities; and why a 10-percent purchase-money mortgage is worth more than a daily double at the racetrack.

Much of what you will read here on investments is very personal. There are so many different methods of putting your money to work that even people who have worked hard at it have not tried all of the different methods. The literature on investing is voluminous, so what we have tried to do is give you tips based upon personal experience in those areas in which we have some experience. The experience of others may be greater, but where we have lost money we have said so, and where we have made it we can sometimes recommend the method to you. Some of our investment preferences will no doubt be criticized, but that's the way life is.

Preference number one is that we like to spend our money where we think we have some knowledge or experience. We recommend this method to you. The best investment is the one you personally know something about. This is not to say that you should not expand your horizons. A few years ago we had never heard of a Eurodollar market; now it is one of our principal investment areas. As for the stock market, we lost so much money in it that now we barely invest in stocks at all.

Many will say our emphasis is wrong. Maybe they are right and we are wrong. We have done very well in the art market; many others, we are sure, would never try it. But that's what this book is all about—the inside view of the rebel investor. We have seen friends of ours who have taken so-called good advice and, today, have nothing to show for it, whereas many of our unorthodox methods have proven to be better for us. In the following chapters we always emphasize the individual—because that's what investment is all about.

2

MANAGING YOUR MONEY—
THE KEY TO SURVIVAL

CAN YOU SAVE YOUR WAY TO WEALTH?

Growing up, we used to hear a lot about saving money. To people of our parents' generation it seemed that there were two kinds of people: Those who spent everything they earned and those who saved as much money as they could.

Although today's world has changed in almost every other way, most people's attitude toward saving money is the same as the previous generation: Put that money away and somehow everything will work out. Unfortunately, it's just not that simple. Saving is not the answer to financial security.

A recent savings bank advertisement shows a man sitting proudly in a chauffeur-driven limousine, billed as "The small saver grown big." Whether it is possible for the small saver to reach those heights is, however, very questionable.

Suppose that a twenty-five-year-old man earning $20,000 a year saved 5 percent of his income ($1000 a year), and that he accumulated interest at 4½ percent. By age sixty-five he would have amassed $112,500—not very much money by today's standards for a lifetime's work.

The two key elements are the amount he can save each year and the interest earned. The rate of interest as the key element to the accumulation of wealth is beyond dispute. Study and memorize Table 1; it's probably the most important thing you can ever learn about investing.

TABLE 1

Investing $1000 a Year and Reinvesting the Income

Rate of Interest	Number of Years Required to Reach $1 Million Without Tax	Amount Accumulated Over 40 Years Without Tax
3 percent	110	$ 77,000
4½ percent	87	112,200
6 percent	70	164,000
8 percent	57	280,000
10 percent	48	487,000
12 percent	42	859,000

As you can see from the table, if you could save $5000 a year at 10 percent instead of $1000 a year at 10 percent, you could accumulate $1 million in one-fifth the time. However, there are two very important factors that you must face— inflation and taxation.

To match a million dollars in terms of its value in 1919, when World War I ended, would require $4.8 million today; a million in 1928 would be the equivalent of approximately $3.2 million to- day; a million in 1948 would equal $2.2 million in the currency of the mid-1970s. And our calcula- tions do not take in the last two years, when in- flation has been horrendous.

As for taxes, most of the Super-Rich fortunes stem from the golden age of little or no taxes. The Rockefellers, the Mellons and the Du Ponts were all helped immensely by the lack of taxes, and there is no question that taxes still play a large part in the accumulation of wealth, as much for the Super-Rich as those in the ordinary-rich category. It was interesting to see how little real taxes former Vice President Rockefeller or former President Nixon paid before they were subject to such scrutiny by the press. Now, of course, all politicians pay more taxes because it looks good to the public. The truth is, however, that the rich generally pay less tax, percentage-wise, because they understand the game and can hire the best lawyers and accountants. For the not-yet rich, taxes today are a calculation, like inflation, that makes a very big difference in the accumulation of wealth.

In sum, while we don't believe that you can save your way to wealth the way the ads say, we do believe that you can get there quicker if you understand the difference that yield or rate plays in the accumulation of money.

KNOW HOW TO BORROW, BUT BORROW WISELY!

It's very hard to convince people that to get ahead they must know how to borrow money wisely. Most people who borrow money use their credit in nonproductive ways, while nonborrowers believe that borrowing money is bad. This latter group regards getting into debt as an act akin to sin. Probably the only time the nonborrowers succumb to borrowing is in connection with purchasing a home, and then they alleviate their anxieties by calling their debt a mortgage.

The fact is that borrowing money, with today's rate of inflation, is often the most effective way to make your money work most efficiently for you as an individual. The wise use of credit can materially aid you in managing your personal finances. But borrowing is like anything else; if you use it correctly, it's a great advantage, but it can be very dangerous if it's not used well.

Before you decide to borrow money, you should assess your own financial situation as objectively as you can. Ask yourself: Do I know how to borrow money? Can I afford to go into debt? For what purpose am I borrowing the money? Only in the light of your answers to these questions should you go shopping for a loan. And before finally deciding to take the loan, make sure that you are acquainted with the real cost of the loan, the criteria lenders use to determine whether or not you are a good risk, the various sources of loans and the types of lenders you should avoid.

The oldest joke about credit is that money is only lent to those people who don't need it in the first place. Basically, the joke is true. Banks and other financial institutions are in the business of lending money for profit. They charge interest, which represents their profit margin on their principal, which is the money they loan to you. It's not hard to understand that they would not be in business very long if they made loans that resulted in the loss of their principal. They must, therefore, make sure that what they loan will be repaid. The first question any banker will ask himself is: Am I likely to be repaid? In a sense, how you answer that question for yourself will determine whether or not you become a successful borrower.

There are as many ways to borrow money as there are ways to invest it, but in essence, you are as good as your word. If you have a clean record

—a record of keeping your promises—then there is no reason why you can't borrow.

Undoubtedly the easiest way to borrow money is on a secured basis, which means that you are borrowing money against some form of security. The security you post could be your home, your savings account, insurance policies, securities or a dozen other forms of collateral. The hardest way to borrow large sums of money is on an unsecured basis. Interestingly, one of the easiest ways to borrow small sums up to $5000 is on an unsecured personal loan basis.

Trying to teach someone to borrow is like trying to teach someone to walk; it's such a basic experience that once you understand it you will wonder why you always thought it so complicated, but it's something that you must go out and do yourself. The best way to learn the rules of borrowing is through actual experience. The important point is that if you have an idea, and think you need to borrow money to put your idea to the test and make it work, then think the whole thing through and put it to your banker. Remember that it is his job to lend money and if the idea makes sense he will probably show you how the financing can be arranged. What you must do is learn from others and always try hard.

This may sound oversimple, but if you look around you, you'll recognize that we are a nation of borrowers; the problem with most people is simply that they get into debt for the wrong reasons. Borrowing to make money, borrowing to increase your return on your investments, borrowing because certain amounts of interest are tax deductible, are all worthwhile reasons for borrowing money. Borrowing to overextend your lifestyle is the beginning of the end for any borrower and could eventually land you in the bankruptcy courts rather than on the proverbial Easy Street.

We are great believers in the use of credit. Indeed in today's environment we see no way to stay ahead of inflation unless you understand the use of other people's money. Look to your bank and recognize that the bank is there to serve your financial needs, not just as a depositor or the holder of a savings account but also as the best and cheapest source of credit. It's amazing to us as we talk to people about the proper use of money how little they know about a system that is vital to a proper understanding of investment.

People who read this book will generally fall into three categories. First, those who can't get credit because they have abused the privilege by borrowing money for things they didn't really need and not repaying it on time, or otherwise not keeping their promises to their lenders. For those people there is little that we can advise except to start again in a small way and build a new, clean record.

Then there are those people who believe in Polonius's advice to his son in Shakespeare's play *Hamlet*: "Neither a borrower nor a lender be." These people probably feel guilty about the very thought of borrowing money. To them it represents some form of weakness in one's character— why should I have to borrow money when I can stand on my own two feet? It should be understood that borrowing money and establishing credit have nothing to do with a person's character or how good a person he is. Being in debt is not a mark of weakness, nor is it a degrading situation. Such notions stem from people's guilt and lack of knowledge about finance, and sometimes from personal family history. As so many of our parents have been quick to say: "I remember the Depression and what happened to you if you owed money." Those days are long gone. Don't be afraid to borrow if it is good business to do so. And today it certainly does make sense to borrow when opportunities arise.

The third group of readers are those people who have learned how to borrow money but generally do it for the wrong reasons. It's for the extra car, color television set, holiday or hundreds of other attractive reasons. We're not saying that it's not right to borrow for these kinds of assets, but what you must realize is that you are giving up your future income in order to have the use of something you want, but don't necessarily need today. Furthermore, you are paying for that privilege at a comparatively high interest rate. For us, that kind of borrowing is the worst kind. It adds to your costs and in most cases doesn't improve your real life-style. What we suggest is a different kind of borrowing: credit to be used to make money; credit to improve the return on your investments; credit to give you the chance to pull ahead of the pack by the proper management of what you have. Think again about the reasons for borrowing and realize how that same income can be used to build a real line of credit—credit to invest and not to spend.

CONTROLLING YOUR SPENDING

"The rich are different from you and me," said F. Scott Fitzgerald. "Yes," retorted Ernest Hemingway, "they have more money." Hemingway could well have added that the rich are also different because they spend more money, and spend more time thinking about money!

One characteristic that distinguishes most of the rich people of our acquaintance is that they spend a good deal of time and energy trying to figure out how they can better manage their money and how they can finance their day-to-day needs as well as their long-term aspirations—an important clue perhaps to how the rich get rich and, more important, stay rich.

Even very rich people, however, don't put off their personal affairs with the excuse that business must come first. Instead, they find the time to do both. For example, the very rich Rockefeller brothers probably spend as much time and energy handling and thinking about the management of the family fortune as they spend on their individual careers. Hence, the Rockefeller family fortune is probably one of the best-managed personal mutual funds in the world.

But even if you aren't a Rockefeller, you do have an income and you do pay taxes, and an understanding of how to manage both is fundamental to the art of living rich.

Income, for tax purposes, is the money you have coming in on a cash basis. This is actual cash received, not cash promised. Individuals, unlike corporations, operate on a strictly cash basis, not an "accrual" basis (more of that later), which means that when you're calculating your income for a particular tax year you only include the money you have actually received, not money that is owing to you.

Suppose that you invested $50,000 with the Chemical Bank in a bank certificate of deposit on February 1, 1977, for one year at the rate of 6½

percent per year. On January 31, 1978, you will
get your $50,000 returned to you plus $3250
representing the interest paid by the bank on the
certificate of deposit. But, since the tax year ended
on December 31, 1977—before the bank had paid
you the $3250—you would report no interest in-
come for the tax year 1977, even though you had
$50,000 in the bank for eleven months of the
year. Instead, you would report that $3250 as
interest income for the tax year ending December
31, 1978, even though it had only been in the
bank for one month of that year.

Obviously, if your income in 1978 is going to be
exactly the same as it was in 1977, there is no real
advantage in managing your tax this way. But if
your earnings fluctuate, and you know you have
a year of low earnings coming up, there is every
advantage. Suppose you are a stockbroker about
to make an extra $25,000 on one deal in 1978,
and plan to spend the next five years working on
your next deal. It makes much more sense to
arrange a deal whereby you'd get $5000 a year for
the next five years, on which you'll pay less tax,
than to have the whole $25,000 in 1978, on which
you'll pay more tax.

But to go back to that $50,000 you had invested
in the Chemical Bank at 6½ percent. On an
"accrual" basis for 1977, you would have eleven-
twelfths of $3250 as "accrued" income and in
1978 you would have one-twelfth of $3250 as
"accrued" income. In theory, on an "accrual" basis,
this eleven-twelfths of $3250 is yours to spend,
but in practice, certificates of deposit are repaid
at the end of the time period, so you won't be able
to spend your accrued income until you actually
receive the cash in hand on the 31st of January

1978. The important lesson to learn from this is to distinguish between what you have coming to you and what you actually have on hand to spend now. It's the difference between having money in your pocket and having no money in your pocket.

With this in mind, it is evident that everyone must have a personal financial plan to get ahead and stay ahead of both the bill collectors and Internal Revenue. Without such a plan, it is impossible to know where you are from week to week or even from year to year. You might devise a simple budget plan as outlined in Table 2.

TABLE 2

For Period Ending

_____

Taxable Income:
Salaries
Interest on Deposits
Dividends
Other Income
Capital Gains*   _____

                                          $

Non-Taxable Income:
Accrued Interest
Accrued Dividends   _____
Other $

        Spendable   •
            Income   Total $_____

* These may be eliminated if President Carter's proposed new tax bill passes Congress.

Taxable Deductions:
Interest Payments
Taxes Paid:
  Real estate,
  personal property,
  state and local
  income, etc.
Business Expenses
Charitable
  Contributions
Legal and
  Accounting Fees
Other
                         _____
                      $

*Personal Non-
Deductible Expenses:*
Estimate of Taxes
  to be Paid
Personal Living
  Expenses:
  Housing, food,
  transportation,
  medical care,
  vacations
  education, etc.
                         _____
                      $

         Spendable
         Disbursements   Total $_____
         Net Spendable

SUMMARY:
(1) Taxable Income $_____
    Less: Taxable
      Deductions   −_____

Amount on
which taxes
are to be paid $_____

(2) Spendable
income $_____
Less: Spendable
Disbursements   –_____
Amount avail-
able to spend
(Net Spend-
able) $_____

(3) Taxable Income $_____
Less Taxable
Deductions
and Personal
Non-deducti-
ble Expenses   –_____
Cash Income to
Spend $_____

A simple budget like this should provide you
with a clear idea of where you are going. By
filling in the amounts you received and spent,
you are actually creating a profit-and-loss statement, both on a cash basis and on an accrual
basis. By dividing each category by 12, for the
months of the year, it becomes a monthly financial plan; divided by 52, it becomes a weekly plan,
should you require that kind of running budget.

Such a financial plan can tell you at a glance:

1. Where your money is coming from
2. What money is subject to tax and what
money is nondeductible

3. What money you have to spend so that you can consider your financial priorities

4. How your spending relates to your own financial security

If your net spending (total spendable income less total spendable disbursements) is in the red, then it is only a question of time until you exhaust your capital. As a minimum, you should try to spend at least no more money than you indicate as net spendable. Although money is earned to be spent, bankruptcy looms for those people who spend more than their net spendable. Remember Dickens's Mr. Micawber: "Annual income twenty pounds, annual expenditure nineteen pounds nineteen shillings and sixpence, result happiness. Annual income twenty pounds, annual expenditure twenty pounds out and sixpence, result misery."

To Mr. Micawber, inflation was something that had to do with blowing up balloons at Christmastime. Today it is your silent partner, eating away at your capital at a rate of between 6 percent and 30 percent, depending on whether you live in a stable economy like West Germany or the United States or a banana republic like Argentina or Nicaragua.

As an individual, there is little you can do about inflation except to ensure that you don't spend all of your net spendable but instead add to your capital, on which you then maximize your returns as some kind of hedge against inflation. It's like the Red Queen in *Through the Looking Glass*, running hard to stay where you are. You should never dip into your capital because once the money is spent you are back to zero, with no hedge against inflation and a diminishing source of income.

When you spend money, you should realize that you are actually buying more than just material things. You are making decisions through your choice of purchases that determine your way of life. These decisions can bring you closer to—or further away from—your personal aspirations about the way you want to live. Money is not just currency; it is a system that translates itself into the way you live and the decisions that will affect your existence.

3

DO YOU HAVE THE PERSONALITY TO LIVE RICH?

It seems that we know a lot of people who spend a lot of money. If you look at the statistics, you wonder where they come from. But, as Russell Baker said in his very funny column entitled "The Phantom Rich," it seems likely that government figures give no real idea of the true wealth of Americans or how widely American wealth is spread. The mystery is who are all these seemingly wealthy people?

We decided to sit down and make a list of the rich people we knew and to see if they had personality characteristics which we could isolate, using Hans Eysenck and Glenn Wilson's *Know Your Own Personality* (London: Temple Smith, 1975) as a guide. Well, we decided they all shared certain qualities and found that they were *active, sociable, risk-takers*. How would you compare yourself to this description?

ACTIVITY

One of the primary traits that distinguish the rich from the not-so-rich is their love of activity. Of course, there are exceptions—the idle rich who get up late and find it a real effort to get themselves to a luncheon date on time—but on the whole, rich people enjoy all forms of activity and invest everything they do with the same driving energy, whether it's running a business, having fun or keeping themselves young, fit and attractive.

Age is no barrier. Just look at Mrs. William Woodward. Although she is in her eighties, she is always impeccably dressed, in excellent physical condition, and can often be seen making the rounds of New York late spots with such varied friends as author Patrick O'Higgins, real-estate investor Jerome Zipkin and artist Andy Warhol. When everyone else is stiffling yawns and watching the clock, it is Elsie who is ready to move on to the next party.

Rich people tend to work hard at whatever they do. They bring the same energy and enthusiasm that they devote to their business or to charity work to their vacations. Not for them the "three-week-catnap-on-the-beach" type of holiday. Their holidays usually involve active sports like skiing, tennis or golf, and they work just as hard and with as much concentration with their ski or tennis instructors as they do with their colleagues in the boardroom. Anyone who has been on a serious skiing holiday can attest to the fact that getting up early, lugging heavy skis while weighted down with heavy ski boots, waiting on lift lines or fighting your way through a cafeteria on the slopes is sheer hard work—and that's not including the mental and physical energy required to parallel down the slopes.

Take ace jet-setter Gunther Sachs, who graces St. Moritz with his presence every winter. Decked out, usually, in an all black ski suit accentuated by an Isadora Duncan–length striped scarf, he arrives fairly early in the morning—eleven o'clock —at the top of the Corviglia ski lift, ready to ski for a couple of hours before adjourning to the

exclusive Corviglia Club for lunch. Invariably he
has been up late the night before either hosting a
party himself or attending a dinner at one of the
privately owned chalets in Suvretta, followed by
a few hours of dancing into the early morning
hours at the Dracula Club he founded in the town.

If all of this energy is not enough to frighten
off an Olympic competitor, Mr. Sachs pushes on
in the afternoon with a bit of tobogganing down
the three-quarter-mile, near-suicidal Cresta Run
that has already claimed three lives. Following
the flirtation with death on the icy run, he can be
found holding court at late afternoon tea in the
lobby of the Palace Hotel. At the Palace, he has
his own personally decorated tower apartment,
complete with a kitchen wallpapered with Andy
Warhol's serigraphs of Marilyn Monroe, a drawing room featuring a flock of lifesize lambs by the
sculptor Lalanne, a three-panel luminous multiple
by Wesselmann of *The Great American Nude*,
and assorted works by Arman, César, Fahri and
Pavlos, to make sure that Mr. Sachs, his beautiful
wife, Mirja, and their young son feel at home even
though they are "roughing it" in a hotel.

Teatime is followed by a few rounds of back-
gammon before he retires to his tower to prepare
for the evening ahead, when the casualty rate is
sometimes even higher than the daytime one,
though the injuries tend to be sore heads and
sheer exhaustion rather than broken legs.

Some celebrities make equally efficient use of
their workdays, too.

City Councilman, former publisher of the *Village Voice* and until recently one of New York's
most sought after bachelors, Carter Burden tries
to find time every day to take an hour of gym-
nastics with the Russian expert Alex, of Alex &

Walter's Physical Fitness Studio on West 57th Street.

Artist Andy Warhol saves time by eating at the Automat or while sitting in front of his television.

William F. Buckley, editor and publisher of the *National Review*, typed his recent novel, *Saving the Queen*, while drinking his morning coffee and riding to work in the back of his chauffeur-driven limousine.

To save vital seconds while on holidays, Ira Howard Levy, senior vice president, corporate marketing design, of Estée Lauder, Inc., travels with pretyped labels bearing the names and address of his friends to stick onto postcards.

There's a whole group of West Coast producers, directors and record company owners who all find time for a set of early morning tennis before going to work, and Don Hewitt, the producer of CBS's award-winning program "Sixty Minutes," has been known to show such an abundance of energy that he was once seen climbing the back stairs of the Britannia Beach Hotel in Nassau, hoping to get a glimpse of Howard Hughes shaving in the bathroom.

There are ten questions that you can ask yourself to find out just how active a person you are:

1. Are you happiest when you are working?
2. If a project calls for fast action, are you stimulated?
3. Do you become restless when working on something that moves at a slow pace?
4. Do you usually finish your meals ahead of other people, even when there is no need to hurry?
5. Do other people regard you as a lively person?

6. Are you always doing something, and never idle?

7. Are you generally very enthusiastic about starting a new project?

8. When you are walking with other people, do they often have difficulty keeping pace with you?

9. Do you like meeting other people?

10. Are you usually full of pep and vigor?

If the answers to all of these questions is yes, then you possess a personality factor indigenous to many people who are living rich.

SOCIABILITY

Being sociable is not necessarily a prerequisite of being rich—Howard Hughes proved that. In fact, in one sense the opposite is true; the major virtue of being antisocial is that it's cheap, so the more of a recluse you become, the more money you can save!

On the whole, however, sociable people are often very successful people because they can bring their personalities to bear on most difficult situations and smooth over many of the rough spots that would discourage or defeat other people. Françoise and Oscar de la Renta, interior designer and clothing designer respectively, are one couple who can be out almost every evening of the week furthering their friendships and their careers by attending parties, dispensing Cat Pack kisses on both cheeks of their chums and adding a little sparkle to every gathering they attend. Mr. and Mrs. Henry J. Heinz so enjoy the company of other people that they often invite various guests, such as art dealer John Richardson and journalist Alan Pryce-Jones, to join them for a Mediterranean cruise on their yacht. And the villas of antique dealers Joe Lombardo and Eddie Harmon are usually full of all manner of friends and acquaintances.

Yuri Arkus-Duntov, investment banker with Allen & Co., is perhaps society's answer to Henry Kissinger. He has so many friends living in most of the major capitals of the world that a typical day in any one of them might include no less than five different appointments for meals, drinks and business with any number of assorted titled royalty and international notables.

Bill Paley, the chairman of the board of CBS, according to Robert Metz's book *CBS: Reflections in a Bloodshot Eye*, so dislikes being alone that "back in the late 1960s he even had his chauffeur drive his $15,000 Maserati Quattroporte, a sleek sedan favored by driving afficionados. That, says one car-loving ex-aide, 'is like having someone else screw your mistress.'"

Simone and Bill Levitt used to so enjoy having people around them that they sometimes authorized Earl Blackwell to invite total strangers to join them on a cruise aboard their former $16-million yacht, *La Belle Simone*.

Among the international party-givers, when people like the Baron de Rédé, Marie-Hélène de Rothschild and Sao Schlumberger give parties their guest lists run into the hundreds and their party costs for food, drink and decorations run as high as the price of a Mediterranean villa.

Here are some questions to determine if you are a social person:

1. Do you like to go out a great deal?
2. Do you often find that friends cheer you up?
3. Are you talkative when with other people?
4. Can you usually let yourself go and have a good time at a party?
5. Do you really enjoy talking to other people?
6. Are you relaxed and self-confident in the company of other people?
7. Do you easily make friends with members of the opposite sex?
8. Do you enjoy playing with young children?
9. Is it important to you that people like you?
10. Do you spontaneously introduce yourself to strangers at social gatherings?
11. Do you like to be in the middle of things?
12. Do you prefer to take your vacation alone or with someone else?

Sociability is an integral part of living rich. If you're trying to do it at no cost, then it's how you get your share—free dinners, free holidays, free theater tickets—and if you're picking up the tab, then entertaining lavishly is one sure way of making people think you are rich.

RISK-TAKING

The third trait you find in people who live rich is that most of them are risk-takers. This is also a common trait among people who are activists, wheeler-dealers and anyone who wants to make a great deal of money.

People like Baron Marcel Bich, Charles Bluhdorn, Sir Charles Clore, Helen Gurley Brown and her husband, producer David Brown, David Frost, Stanley Goldblum, Sir James Goldsmith, the late Jimmy Hoffa, Claes Oldenburg, Sir Max Joseph, John King, Saul Steinberg, Jim Ling, Frank Lloyd and Jack Paar all live fairly dangerously and, like gamblers, take enormous business risks with seeming unconcern for the potentially disastrous consequences. They all share a common conviction, though—they all believe in themselves rather than "luck." They believe they can control the odds because of their knowledge and strength of character. The risk-taking goes hand in hand with "impulsiveness" and "tough-mindedness" and they get their kicks from negotiating big deals involving risk but revolving around their own abilities.

Are you a risk-taker?

1. Would you prefer a job involving change, travel and variety, even if it was risky and insecure?

2. Do you enjoy taking risks?

3. When the odds are against you, do you still really think it worth taking a chance?

4. Would life with no danger in it be too dull for you?

5. Do you like to gamble?

If you answered yes to all three series of questions, you can assume that you are an active, sociable risk-taker—a fine candidate for living rich and enjoying it. Among the group that lives rich there are some individuals who profess to prefer to live simply, quietly and modestly. Perhaps a couple of them really mean it, but for the most part, just take away some of the rich trappings of their way of life and you'll find them hollering. For some unknown reason—perhaps guilt—many people who have virtually everything feel a need to claim that they really don't want what they have. It's unfortunate for these people that they fail to come to terms with their lives. If you've got it, then enjoy it!

4

HOW DO THE RICH LIVE?

LEARN FROM OTHERS

Spending money is an activity that most people take for granted. As we've said before, it's not how much you have but how you spend it that really counts in the end. To illustrate the point, we thought it might be fun to look at other people and see what they do with their money. There are many lessons to be learned—both positive and negative—by looking at other people.

We want people to start thinking about the way they live and to realize that it's not the quantity you spend that counts but the quality of your lifestyle that determines how successfully you live. This is the essence of living rich.

DOES MONEY REALLY GROW ON TREES?

Here's an example of a New York couple who really gave the impression of having the original money tree right in their fashionable East Side backyard.

For the sake of anonymity, let's call them Stan and Beverly King. They are both in their middle thirties, in good physical health and engaged in the active pursuit of recognition. Stan came from a wealthy, relatively unknown Eastern family.

The only son of indulgent parents, he tried his hand at a variety of careers, including a stint as a theatrical agent. One day an attractive, stage-struck girl from the West Coast came into his office looking for help with her show business ambitions. One thing led to another, and although Stan never found Beverly a starring role in a Broadway musical, he did manage to take her home to meet his parents. The meeting may not have had the same spectacular outcome as the old-time introductions of gorgeous young girls to the late Flo Ziegfeld, but in its own way, it proved to be a propitious occasion.

Beverly set about helping Stan launch himself in a distinguished profession. They married, bought a $250,000 townhouse on New York's fashionable East Side, put Stanley into the antiques business with an inventory estimated at one million dollars, and set about building a reputation as two of New York's youngest "Beautiful People," something which is hard to do for less than $150,000 a year—all in the supposed interest of furthering Stan's antique business. Their house became his showroom and their perpetual socializing and relentless pursuit of new acquaintances among the world's jet set were justified as a means of meeting the right people who could afford to buy what Stan had to sell.

In the meantime, Beverly and Stan produced a child and Beverly went out to work for a famous jewelry designer as a combination showroom manager and social public relations person. The designer's work was always avant garde and received constant attention in the press, with many of the stories featuring Mrs. Stanley King describing this or that—or Mrs. Stanley King wearing

52-karats-worth of diamonds and emeralds to an afternoon charity luncheon.

Their life-style was dazzling and obviously very costly. They moved from one townhouse to another of twice the size and at least twice the value and subsequent taxes. Beverly's clothing budget— at least $50,000 a year—could have fed half the starving Biafran children. Couture clothes by Mme. Grès and Chloë were an annual acquisition. Sonia Rykiels, St. Laurents and other costly ready-to-wear were acquired with a fervor that usually accompanies religious devotion. The clothes were accessorized with every imaginable fur, cut into the trendiest shape of the moment, and the whole ensemble was set aglitter with Bulgari evening bags, and dazzling rings and earrings and necklaces from David Webb, Bulgari and other jewelers of equal distinction. To make sure that everyone knew just how chic and attractive they were, they engaged the services of one of the all-time great public relations men and justified it as a business expenditure for the sake of selling antiques; but most of the press releases concerning the Kings were based on their latest social doing.

With their city image secure during the winter months, they tried their hand at achieving equal social success in the glamorous summer resorts. A stint in the Caribbean served to introduce them to little more than exiled alcoholics and 100 percent humidity, which only frizzed Beverly's diligent coiffure. A foray to the Hamptons proved equally disappointing. Their rented house was at the end of a cow pasture and proved the favored meeting place of the biggest horse flies on Long Island.

Beverly quit her job with the jewelry designer

and decided to resume her theatrical ambitions. Desirous of the recognition achieved by Barbara Walters and other television interviewers, she opted this time for a career in television. She practiced her speech and seemed glued to the television, watching the varied performances of female interviewers and commentators on the three major networks. Every morning she spent an hour exercising to stay slim and shapely for the cameras and then used much of the rest of her day cultivating friendships with female friends, many of whom had positions with fashion magazines, retail and cosmetic companies or in television, in the hope that she might get her first big break. She worked hard at improving her performance and made the rounds of casting directors at many advertising agencies and companies with untiring application.

Needing a holiday from their demanding lifestyle, Beverly and Stan decided to exhibit at one of the European antique fairs and use the exhibition as an excuse to travel through Europe for ten weeks, in a style which cost at least $5,000 a week, spending the last month of the trip in a rental villa on the French Riviera, which had to cost almost another $10,000. They arrived at Nice Airport with a mountain of luggage and a little black book filled with names and telephone numbers of anyone and everyone "worthwhile" who had been referred to them back home by friends, acquaintances and their publicist. They spent their days working the various beach resorts up and down the coast, looking for new international jet set friends. In the evenings, they attended every cocktail party in Monte Carlo's Hotel de Paris and Hermitage, hosted by various jewelry and fashion designers to lure the local vacationers into a little impulse shopping. They ate hors d'oeuvres and sipped champagne with the local managers of Bulgari, Cartier, Van Cleef & Arpels, Mr. Fred, Christian Dior, Jean Patou and Lanvin. They befriended some of the long-standing villa owners who were already well ensconced in the social realm, hoping not only to be included on their party guest lists, but also to be invited along with them to parties given by their sociable friends, who always seemed to have expandable guest lists—especially when it was a matter of a young, attractive couple who could enliven the usual dowager-heavy guest list. In their spare time, they worked the cocktail lounges and terraces of the local deluxe hotels, making sure that they left no stones unturned.

To all those who knew them, their life-style seemed to represent the height of lavish expenditure. Their second town house cost at least $500,000 plus another $200,000 or so to renovate and decorate. Their summer holidays complete with European and Middle Eastern sojourns ran at least another $40,000. The taxes on their town house were about $25,000 a year and Beverly's clothing, fur and jewelry budget had to be every bit of $50,000 in one year. Add to this the additional costs of fulltime housekeeping plus daily help, private school fees for their only child, costly insurance for Stanley's stock of expensive antiques plus the various and sundry weekly expenses for special lessons, television pilots, exercise classes, hairdressing, lavish bouquets of flowers, groceries, and all the rest, and you would have an annual total that would consume the gross salary of the president of General Motors. The scale of their

living and its inherent expenses seemed even
more fantastic because it was generally known
that Stan considered it a good year when he sold
one or two antique commodes. Everyone has heard
of generous parents who give their children lots
of money and possessions during their lifetimes
so that they can see their children enjoy themselves, but the expenditures of Beverly and Stanley seemed to exceed even that of the most
indulgent families. In fact, their life-style had
everyone wondering how they managed to sustain
it.

Then, one day, a strange thing happened. After
a couple of months of domestic strife, the Kings
separated and proceeded to divorce. No specific
reasons were cited, but the New York jungle tele-
graph was broadcasting a variety of speculation,
and among the recurring rumors was the theory
of financial indigestion. Here were two young
people who seemed to have the world by its tail.
They had money, possessions, good health and
rich parents. What more could anyone ask? And
yet, with all of this, their story proved the old
lesson that money can't buy happiness.

Furthermore, don't delude yourself about money
growing on trees because even the best tree can
grow barren. Take the case of a well-known
former chairman of a major company who was
eased out after many years. The independent directors, prodded we suppose by the banks and
institutions, decided that he had to go. He soon
resigned his $450,000-a-year-plus job, though the
break was not complete as he was retained as a
consultant for five years at $75,000 a year plus
certain extras. That would probably come down
to $50,000 after taxes.

Before you need to worry about what happens to $50,000 a year after tax, you must—to misquote the most eminent Victorian cook, Mrs. Beaton—first catch your $50,000!

One way is to have about $750,000 to $1 million of real cash net worth, which will yield, after taxes, an annual income of around $50,000 ($850,000 × 9% = $76,500 − tax $26,500 = $50,000 after tax). The other is to work for, or better still own, a company which, in partnership with the government, will pay half your expenses for you. In that case, with the company spending around $10,000 a year on your behalf (and if you don't believe that companies do spend that much on key employees, we envy you your innocence!), you can get by with a salary of around $60,000, yielding $40,000 after taxes. If you have some capital to invest, it certainly would help get you to that magical $50,000 a year after taxes.

Looked at from that angle, the difference between your salary on paper and what it *really* means to be boss, or close to the boss, in real cash terms becomes very clear. Sadly, too many people who run large companies or hold top jobs only realize exactly how much their jobs were worth after they've resigned, retired or been fired, and find themselves having to pay out of their own pockets for things they previously took for granted, like transportation, accommodations, even food and drink. Unless they have a great deal of the company's stock, which they can sell to replace their salaries and perquisites, their standard of living suffers a sharp, often painful decline.

In his years as the top man, we suppose that this particular gentleman had the usual company car and chauffeur, use of the company airplane and other travel paid for, at least in part, by the company, not to mention the suites in luxury hotels and a couple of apartments maintained by the company for his use. No doubt, too, a good deal of entertaining both at home and abroad was paid for out of company funds.

At a very conservative estimate, these extras would have cost him a minimum of $50,000 a year if he had had to pay for them himself. Or, to put it any other way, he would have needed around $1 million invested at 7½ percent, yielding around $75,000 before tax, to leave him with $50,000 to spend after tax! If you also take into consideration the fact that, to equal his salary of $450,000, he would have needed a capital base of $8 million ($8 million invested at 7½ percent would yield $600,000—around $450,000 after tax), you realize that he was not merely losing a job but the equivalent of $9 million in the bank!

How would someone in this position, who now finds himself with $50,000 a year after tax, spend his money? Probably such a person would already own his cooperative apartment at a fashionable address, but he probably has a mortgage or other loan against it for, let's say, about $25,000. Assuming that he can persuade the banks to forget the amortization, the interest cost at 8 percent is still $2,000 a year, plus the apartment's annual maintenance costs which surely run upward of $18,000 ($1500 per month), which brings the cost of running his apartment to at least $20,000. A car, chauffeur, insurance, or just car rental fees, would cost a minimum of $5000 per year. His clothing costs would be figured at $1500 with his wife's clothing costing twice that, at $3000 a year. Spending money, restaurants, household help, medical expenses would come to not less than $150 per week, or $7800 per year. A small place in the country, either owned or rented, costs at least $5000 a year. Two or three vacations during the year, including plane fare, probably figure in the neighborhood of a minimum of $7500.

We have not provided for alimony, child support, and gifts and education, etc., for his children from a former marriage. That would run at least $5000 a year. Nor have we included any potential investments, luxury purchases, art or antiques, or the hidden costs of maintaining a big-city lifestyle. Even so, adding it all up, it's easy to see how he could spend $50,000 a year in no time and not live very extravagantly. Look at any one of the categories outlined in Table 3 and you will see that the costs are not very high. The fact is, it's virtually impossible for a man with such commitments and life-style to live on less.

Of course, people like this are not "average" Americans, but try to find anyone making $50,000 a year pretax, living in a major American city, who can maintain a life-style of comfort and moderate luxury for less than $50,000 a year after tax. (See Table 3)

HOW MUCH MONEY A WIFE CAN SPEND

The wife of a very wealthy man usually spends her time on nonfinancial matters (although she is spending her husband's money). Were she curious about her financial profile, however, it might run like this:

TABLE 3

Expenses	Total	Percent of income
Interest Expenses (mortgages)	$ 2,000	3.94
Maintenance (apartment or houses)	18,000	35.78
Clothing (his and hers)	5,000	10.06
Spending Money ($150 per week)	7,800	6.44
Country House (rental)	5,000	10.06
Vacations	7,500	6.70
Child Support	5,000	10.06
Total	$50,300	

She is probably at least thirty-five years old, although it's getting harder and harder to pinpoint her age. While youth is a commodity that money can't buy, she has discovered that a few thousand dollars invested in plastic surgery and silicone injections are a pretty good substitute.

She has been trying to make the "Best-Dressed List" for years so that her name could be placed alongside those of Babe Paley, Gloria Guinness and Jacqueline Onassis, but Eleanor Lambert and her judges have never even heard of her, let alone recognized her as a clothes-horse. She's probably been written up in the *New York Times* and *Women's Wear Daily* at least twice and she is known to fight her way to the foreground when a *Times* or *WWD* photographer is in sight on the off chance that he will snap her and that the editors will run her photos as the epitome of chic.

If she's really serious about the "Best-Dressed List," she must have a beautifully kept body on which to hang those clothes. To achieve this, she must pick at her veal piccata while lunching at Orsini's, spend at least three mornings a week at exercise class and have at least a once-a-week massage. Periodic holidays at La Costa, the Golden Door or the more spartan English health hydros are another must for keeping it all looking as it should. Many of her more profound observations are probably gleaned from her early morning calisthenics in front of the television set turned to the morning news and talk shows.

Her typical day begins early—perhaps at eight —with breakfast in bed, if she's lucky enough to find someone who will serve it to her. Then, it's onto the floor for bends, stretches, pushes and pulls, with a little television news in between grunts. After thirty minutes of exercise she makes and takes a few telephone calls to and from the usual group of daily pals before heading into the bathtub, which has been filled with enough bath oils and perfumes to keep the cosmetic company stocks selling at record prices.

After a leisurely soak, she'll spend an hour or so on her makeup and attire before she is ready to face the world—or at least that section of it to be found in her hairdresser's salon. Before leaving the house, she might check with the cook on the menus and place some telephone orders for food and flowers.

She will then proceed to the hairdresser for her morning comb-out, essential before she can face the really pressing matters of the day—like lunch at any one of the chic Le or La restaurants running off both sides of Fifth Avenue. Her comb-outs cost about $6 each plus various tips, and are probably booked twice weekly, along with twice-weekly shampoo-and-set appointments ($15 each), a once-a-week manicure ($4), once-a-month cutting and coloring ($50), once-a-month pedicure ($6) and leg wax ($18). As all of the finest salons have no less than three or four people fussing over you for most ministrations, figure the tips at another 20 percent of the bill.

Lunch is usually booked at restaurants like Orsini's, "21," Le Caravelle, La Grenouille and La Goulue, where a low-calorie lunch for two must cost a minimum of $40. After lunch, she probably browses through the nearest department store—Saks, Bonwit's, Bergdorf's, Bendel's or Bloomingdale's—and adds a little something to her already bulging wardrobe before heading home.

Putting together her annual wardrobe is a serious affair. Our archetypal wife spends at least $25,000 per year on clothing—not including furs and jewelry. She buys herself at least two to three pairs of winter boots ($130 each), several pairs of shoes ($60 to $125 each), one Hermès handbag ($650) and assorted "budget" handbags from other shops ranging in price from $80 to $300 each.

Her daytime clothes run the gamut from St. Laurent three-piece ensembles that can be put together for $800 and up, to Missoni knits ($600), Sonia Rykiel separates ($700) and bits and pieces from Valentino, Ungaro, Lapidus and others, where the bits cost at least $100 and the pieces start at $200. Her dinner dresses are probably Jean Muirs ($300 and up) or Christian Dior Boutique $600 and up) or dressier versions of the daytime looks in more luxurious fabrics at proportionately higher prices. Her party clothes and ball gowns come from Chloë ($900 and up and up), St. Laurent ($600 and up), Zandra Rhodes ($800 and up), Holly's Harp ($600 and up) and some of the other American designers like Halston ($600 and up), Oscar de la Renta and Sant'Angelo. Her raincoat is from St. Laurent ($600), her jackets are from him, too, or from Polo or Calvin Klein ($200 to $500) and her two everyday coats cost $500 and up each.

To put together more outfits from her purchases, she collects St. Laurent silk shirts at $220 each, cashmere sweater sets ($110 and up), novelty sweaters ($60 and up), snakeskin belts ($30 each), cashmere gloves and scarves ($50 and up) and various-sized Louis Vuitton shopping bags ($150 and up) to cart home the little purchases that she can't wait to wear.

Her furs come from the name designers like Maximilian who charge $12,000 for a sable coat, and she probably buys one fur piece—either a coat, jacket, cape, fur-lined raincoat, vest or shawl —per year. Little gold hoop earrings in various sizes for sportswear come from Tiffany's or Cartier ($125 and up for the small size), while important pieces come from Van Cleef & Arpels, Bulgari or David Webb. For her birthday she might get a gold and enamel and jeweled minaudière from Bulgari for a modest $7000, while she already has enough gold chains from Hermès and Tiffany's ($300 and up each) to anchor QE II.

Our archetypal American spender goes to Europe at least once a year, and while her husband attends to business she shops and goes to fashion shows, where she spends a small fortune saving money on the foreign-made goods that cost even more in the United States.

Considering the prices of name-designer ready-to-wear, $25,000 per year doesn't go very far. A modest budget would look like this:

6	Daytime outfits (accessorized with belts, scarves, sweaters, shirts)	$4,000
5	Dinner outfits	2,700
5	Party outfits	3,500
3	Ball gowns	3,000
1	Red fox coat	7,500
2	Cloth coats	1,600
1	Raincoat	575
Sportswear:	Bikinis, tennis and golf clothes, slacks, shirts, T shirts, shorts, etc.	1,800
	Ski clothes: Pants and jackets, or salopette and jacket	300
Shoes:	8 pairs	900
Gloves:	8 pairs (always losing them)	200
Boots:	3 pairs	400
Handbags	4–5	1,200
		$27,675

While most of New York's Upper East Side female population appear to be beautifully and expensively dressed and groomed, some of them achieve the same dazzling effects without squandering in one year a sum of money equal to sending a child through twelve years of private school.

The first group of women are those with friends and connections in the so-called rag trade. Either their husbands or they themselves are or were involved in work on Seventh Avenue, or they have or had an editorial or executive position that put them into contact with designers and manufacturers. These women cultivate these friend-ships and work harder at maintaining them than they work at making a successful marriage. The difference between buying wholesale on Seventh Avenue and buying retail on Fifth or Madison avenues is roughly 55 percent. In addition, left-over samples, end-of-season stock, jobber's bar-gain-priced extra dresses eked out of fabric allot-ments, all add up to being well dressed at half the cost.

The system is simple. The women visit the showrooms during the collection shows for the buyers. They look at the samples, select their favorites, pay for them upon receipt of the goods and wear them to lunch and dinner a day or two before they hit the windows of the better shops, creating the illusion that they are, once again, setting the trends.

This wholesale shopping carries over into sports-wear, costume jewelry, handbags and even furs. Therefore these women can cut our basic budget by 50 percent—an astonishing difference in the total sum of money spent to be well dressed.

Also in this category of wholesale shoppers are some of the rich and famous ladies whose names are forever appearing in society columns and fashion magazines. Many designers lend these ladies clothing as well as selling them clothing at wholesale prices to earn the free publicity. The *New York Times*, *Women's Wear Daily* and col-umnists like Suzy, Liz Smith and Eugenia Shep-pard are always reporting who gowned and coiffed which rich and famous lady at last night's hot spot, providing the name designer with free pub-licity worth thousands of dollars. It may seem unfair that these rich and famous ladies receive such favors when they are the very people who are best able to afford designer clothing, but think how many ensembles these ladies need to maintain their best-dressed status. These same ladies also manage one or two trips a year to Europe to shop for clothing at prices far below the price of imports in the United States. Even with U.S. Customs charging them duty for any wholesale purchases above $100, the European shopping spree is still a worthwhile excursion.

There are some women who really lose their heads when it comes to shopping abroad. An example of this was Mrs. Alfred Bloomingdale, a perennially best-dressed jet-setter. Having purchased a few couture dresses from Christian Dior a while back, Betsy Bloomingdale neglected to list them at their accurate valuation on her Customs' form when returning to the United States. The Custom's authorities, no doubt delighted to have snared a big-name luminary, literally made a federal case of it, and Mrs. Bloomingdale, who eventually pleaded guilty in court, just narrowly escaped a prison sentence. International newspaper coverage of the embarrassing scandal probably resulted in hundreds of women suddenly deciding to "go straight" when next faced with a "goods to declare" form.

The other category of women who manage to be well dressed at half the cost encompasses a group of frugal ladies who frequent fashionable discount stores to save money. They browse through the finest stores and thumb through the fashion magazines before heading off to places like Bolton's in New York, Loehmann's in Westchester and the Bronx, Remin's in Westchester, Chutzpah in Great Neck and Palm Beach, and Empire in Riverdale and Long Island. (The really frugal will buy their clothes in New Jersey to avoid New York sales tax.) American designer clothing can be found in these outlet stores at the same time they hang in the department stores, but thrifty shopping can save as much as 20 to 50 percent per item. The racks may be crammed beyond capacity with manufacturers' close-outs, and the dressing rooms are often communal affairs with wall-to-wall bodies, but such conditions have been overlooked by even the likes of Zsa Zsa Gabor, when she was intent on finding a bargain. For Zsa Zsa, of course, Loehmann's managed to clear a dressing room for her exclusive use, but other ladies with pressing social schedules, who have to stretch their husbands' corporate salaries to cover more demanding needs such as educating children, willingly sacrifice comfort, convenience and privacy to acquire a substantial part of their wardrobes in such outlet shops.

On Saturday mornings the same women can be found in the lobbies of buildings on Broadway and Seventh Avenue waiting for elevators to take them up to showrooms that open for Saturday morning cash-only business. If none of the manufacturers sell to the public, or if a woman has no "contact" —no friend who has a cousin who works as a salesman for one of these manufacturers—the best thing to do is ask directions from the crowds on Saturday morning on Broadway or Seventh Avenue or wait for one of the old-timers to tell the elevator operator which floor she wants. Come equipped with cash and you'll always be welcomed. If you can't find a group of shoppers, just ask the elevator starter in one of the fashion buildings who is open for Saturday business; when a few dollars cross his palm, he could provide you with a list of showrooms to keep you busy for a month of Saturdays.

There are also a number of fancy resale shops that will have hardly worn but expensive couturier clothing. Sometimes a wealthy woman must look smashing for a special event, a one-shot extravaganza, and will not be able to wear the same dress again (usually every special event calls for a different dress). In that case, she may sell it to a resale shop to recoup some of her money. She may also get rid of the clothing she no longer wants, as well as her furs, to get ready for next year's models. Places like the Ritz Thrift Shop in Manhattan will have furs that once belonged to the rich and famous. Scouting around (use the Yellow Pages) may turn up more.

LIVING RICH AT HALF THE COST

If there were a Nobel prize to be won for living successfully above your means, then the Countess Christina Paolozzi and her husband, plastic surgeon Howard Bellin, would be odds-on-favorites to win. The secret of their success, you could argue, is an individuality bordering on eccentricity, which means they are always in demand as guests *and* that they can break all the rules of living rich, without anybody caring.

Since they first met, in the early 1960s, they have been providing the gossip columnists with first-class copy. There was the time Christina was photographed in the nude by Richard Avedon for *Harper's Bazaar*. It was the first display of nudity in a fashion magazine, and that, coupled with the fact that Christina was a countess, caused a furor, both public and private. Her mother, who until her marriage to Count Lorenzo Paolozzi was Alice

Spaulding, one of the heirs to the William S. Spaulding and United Fruit Company fortunes, accused Christina of bringing shame on the whole family. Howard, on the other hand, was delighted. "If you've got it," he said, "flaunt it!"

Throughout their marriage there have been a few very minor outrages to keep their names in the minds of the gossip-reading public, culminating in their appearance on Barbara Walter's program, "Not for Women Only." The subject was unconventional marriages, and the Bellins had more than a few *bon mots* to offer on their own brand of marriage American-style. The concept of live-in girl friends and boy friends rounding out the traditional nuclear family had the National Broadcasting Company's telephone wires burning. Christina's mother accused Howard of destroying the fiber of American morality, and the program became a great source of lunch and dinner conversation at all the restaurants and dinner parties.

On paper they seemed a very unlikely couple. Howard comes from a comfortable New Jersey family; his father owned a small department store in West Orange, called Bellin's, which provided the family with everything they needed and paid for Howard's studies at Flower Fifth Avenue Medical School. Christina, on the other hand, sprang from mixed American and European aristocratic stock, and while Howard was studying his way through college and medical school she was receiving a far less formal education in the fashionable resorts of the world.

Despite their vastly different backgrounds, Howard and Christina found a compatability resting on their mutual admiration and a filling of one another's needs. For Howard, Christina's life-style, title and love of the unconventional provided an attractive outlet for his limitless energies and an opportunity to expand his horizons and try his own hand at jet-setting. For Christina, Howard represented stability and a commitment to an ideal. He was, after all, preparing himself for an extremely demanding profession, and yet, at the same time, he seemed perfectly willing not only to cope with her madcap life-style but also to become a willing partner to it.

After a wedding which was attended by a mixed bag of guests including international aristocrats, relatives, actresses and American society figures, they went off to live in Florida while Howard completed his internship and his military service. Christina spent her days in the role of home-maker, trying to create the kind of steady, mundane home-life that was totally new to her, and when their two sons were born, both she and Howard took to parenthood like ducks to water.

Once their stint in Florida was over, Christina's mother made them a wedding gift of a sprawling cooperative apartment with terraces broad enough for the children to ride their bicycles along. Sounds glossy, but because it was high up on Park Avenue the maintenance costs were low, and since it was a gift, they didn't have to cope with mortgages or bank loans.

While Howard completed his residency and started building his practice, Christina set about establishing their names in society. And, again, she did it as much if not more with style as with money. Rarely a week went by without them holding a party. In the daytime it was a steady series of children's parties, celebrating any and all possible occasions that would bring joy to two little boys. And for the grown-ups, family-crested invitations to buffet suppers went out to never less than a hundred people at a time. Everyone (who was anyone) eventually found their way to the Bellins' soirees and the guest list often included the likes of Christina Onassis, Cindy and Joey Adams, the first Mrs. Moshe Dayan, Bunky and Camilla Sparv Hoover, Margaux Hemingway, actress Ina Balin and a wide cross section of any cultural, political and royal notables who happened to be in town.

As their social reputation blossomed, so did Howard's career. Of course his skill as a plastic surgeon had a great deal to do with it, but in the upper echelons of medicine, particularly in an area like plastic surgery, you have to be not merely good but also fashionable. Being featured regularly in the society pages *and* meeting the rich and would-be beautiful people socially did Howard's career no harm at all.

While all the above makes their life-style sound almost too sybaritic, the one other important quality that endears them to many people is their extreme generosity—with their time and talents as well as with money. When the Six-Day War in Israel broke out, Howard took the first plane out and spent the war sewing up wounded Israeli soldiers. When there were earthquakes in Guatemala and Nicaragua, and civil war in Biafra, Howard immediately dropped everything and went to help. Christina devotes a lot of her time to the children's wards in the hospitals where Howard works, and she also helps Vietnamese war victims.

Howard owns and flies his own King Air, after a brief flirtation with helicopters which came to an end when friends invited him to drop in one day and he did, literally, right into their prized seventy-five-year-old oak tree. The Bellins are always to be seen in the most fashionable resorts at the right time of year—the south of France and Fire Island in the summer, Rome or St. Thomas for Christmas.

Christina usually gives everyone some warning of their whereabouts with an occasional newsletter that she dispatches to friends and relations listing some of their recent holidays along with their plans for future ones. One woman was taken aback when she received Christina's newsletter and learned that the Bellin entourage was about to descend upon *her* for a spring holiday—uninvited!

When you invite Christina for a holiday, not only does she come but she stays for a very long time and often invites other friends to come for lunch, dinner or drinks, and, before you know it, your house has more activity than the Eden Roc at the height of the season. Everyone puts up with it, though, because of the Bellins' own generosity and conviviality. Howard usually turns up as a houseguest when we are in the south of France each summer, but the Bellins have repeatedly offered us their guest room whenever we're in New York. The fact that we don't choose to take them up on their kind offer is our fault.

If you invite them to dinner, chances are that they will turn up with a boy friend and a girl friend in tow, which can be very disconcerting for the hostess if she's catered for a specific number and carefully worked out her seating plan. But we also know that neither Christina nor Howard would bat an eyelid if we arrived for dinner at their home with boy friends, girl friends *and* their respective wives and husbands in tow!

Their life-style suggests that they must be extremely rich, and, obviously, to live the way the Bellins live does require some money. But not as much as you might think.

Their apartment, modest by high-flying New York standards, was a gift, but their monthly maintenance charges are approximately $800. Howard drives a $22,000 Pentara automobile, while Christina drives a $6000 station wagon, both of which get garaged for a total of $160 per month. They have two maids for about $250 a week, and both children attend private school, with a total annual tuition bill of $5000. Recent repairs and redecorating at the apartment (many of which were genuinely necessary) ran about $28,000. Clothing for Christina, Howard and the children runs about $10,000 per year. Christina is not a clotheshorse; although she does occasionally buy some ready-to-wear things in Paris, she wears mostly jeans or funky, put-together ensembles. She does not buy a lot of jewelry or expensive furs.

A large part of their budget is spent on vacations, and then mostly on air fares. They usually take two weeks together in the summertime in the south of France with the children. While there, they might take one or two brief trips to Italy. Then Howard usually stays on with friends, while Christina flies back to New York where she usually rents a house on Fire Island for the summer for approximately $3000.

At Christmas they sometimes fly to her mother's house in St. Thomas, and during the rest of the year they often take weekend trips or other brief holidays with his plane, visiting places like the historic restoration at Williamsburg with the children, spending a few days in the sun in Florida, skiing in the Northeast, or paying visits to friends.

But Howard recoups a large part of the cost of running the plane by chartering it to corporations when he isn't using it, and most of their jet-setting is done on the cheap. Christina's mother owns houses in Rome as well as St. Thomas, so they save on hotel costs, and in the south of France they often stay with friends as houseguests. When they stay in the expensive hotels, they have been known to ask that two beds be put into their room for the children. Because they are the Bellins, however, no one thinks business must be bad for Howard, or considers crossing them off their cocktail-party list.

LIVING RICH AT NO COST

If you have no money but are convinced that you have a vast untapped talent for living rich, then there is one very important fact that you should grasp right at the beginning: Just because a man is rich does not mean that his friends are automatically fascinating, glamorous or extremely good company. What it does often mean is that he is prepared—to put it crudely—to *buy* good company. At the most modest level, he may do so with an expensive gourmet dinner; going up the scale, with invitations to Mediterranean cruises on private yachts, or holidays on Caribbean islands, all expenses paid.

Of course you must have something to offer in return—a reputation, perhaps, made with a novel

that has all the critics jumping or an extremely
fashionable art exhibition, or a name or face that
the public (or at least the section of it that con-
cerns your host) recognizes easily. You may be a
TV reporter or a magazine editor, an up-and-
coming interior designer, or even *the* current
astrologer—as long as it's interesting and as long
as it's thought glamorous, it doesn't matter too
much what you do.

Obviously, if you are an extremely amusing
raconteur, that's an added bonus, but often just
being there is all that's asked of you. Fame by
association, that's the theory. If you, the most
talked-about young novelist in New York, spend a
holiday in John Doe's house on Cap d'Antibes,
then John Doe must be a pretty cultured, interesting guy to have you as a friend. At least that's
what he hopes people are going to think!

There are a considerable number of people who
live very successfully above their means this way.
They are always invited to the chic gatherings,
they're present at every museum opening, gallery
showing, resort premiere. Their dining in the
right places is reported along with what they wore
and what they had to say, and their opinions on
everything ranging from gardening to the manner
of painting one's walls becomes gospel that is believed and heeded in some of the wealthiest homes
in the world. For them, influence and position is
a very acceptable substitute for money, though
the people who try to convert that particular currency often find that it isn't that easily convertible.

Take Marion Javits, wife of an important senior
senator, and Superlady about New York.

For a while is seemed that Marion Javits had an
almost magnetic effect on money. Where she was,

vast quantities of it seemed to collect. As an "instant" vice president of Ruder & Finn, super public-relations agents, she got a big new $500,000 account for the company and a $67,500 fee as well as a title on the door for herself. It seems that the Javit's friendship with the sister of the shah of Iran had paid off for all concerned except for the senator, who was considerably embarrassed and insisted that his wife give up the fee, the job and the account, in that order.

Anita Hachette, estranged wife of Jean-Louis Hachette (of the huge French publishing empire), decided that the only point to having an active social life is making it pay. When she started work for the top Parisian auctioneers, she gave a cocktail party, preceding an important sale, for all her society friends and, hopefully, potential customers of the firm. For her it was the ideal way of killing two birds with one stone. "It's fun to have three hundred people for drinks, but nobody can afford it anymore!" Unless you combine business with pleasure, that is.

Her flamboyance, complete with floor-length minks and gigantic hats, means that she is always in demand as a guest at any function where publicity would not be unwelcome, whether a charity ball or private function held by socially ambitious people.

People like Anita Hachette are courted by the rich not simply for their interesting and amusing company but for their ability to impart fame. Remember Baby Jane Holzer, who rose to overnight fame in the 1960s. Who was she, after all, but an attractive New York socialite married to a wealthy young man named Leonard Holzer? But Diana Vreeland loved her look, and before you could say "instant stardom" her face was on the cover of

Vogue, Andy Warhol was doing her portrait, windowsful of Saks Fifth Avenue mannequins were sporting her face and flowing mane of hair, and Tom Wolfe was writing books about her. The girl couldn't go to dinner, catch a cold or discover a new boutique without it being reported by the *New York Times*, *Women's Wear Daily*, and the *New York Post*.

Jane Holzer had money, looks and position, but that alone could not have made her the cult figure she became. Her greatest asset was a circle of friends and acquaintances in the fields of fashion, art and the media who found her attractive and amusing and were in a position to tell the rest of America so.

In Baby Jane's case, fame cost nothing, but it's possible to hire someone, if you have the money, to make you famous. Look at other cult figures of the last ten years—Twiggy, say, or Margaux Hemingway. To all intents and purposes they burst onto the scene overnight, but behind that "instant" fame was a lot of hard work and skillful manipulating—in Twiggy's case by her manager, Justin de Villeneuve, and in Margaux Hemingway's, Errol Wetson, who also married her.

There is also another way to live rich at little or no cost. It's called knowing the right public-relations man.

Since the rich and the celebrated are news, the public-relations departments of many companies, hotels and restaurants have decided that the best way to promote an event is to fly a planeload of rich socialites, celebrities, movie stars, oil magnates, sheiks, titled-but-poor Europeans, pop personalities, hairdressers, dress designers, interior designers, and whomever else they think passes for international society in this increasingly demo-

cratic era, to some great event to ensure publicity.
What guarantees the attendance of most of these
illustrious personages is the fact that jet-setters
will fly anywhere as long as someone else is picking up the tab!

Organizing these airborne circuses is a string
of clever public-relations people, like Colonel Serge
Obolensky, Earl Blackwell and Paris's Yanou Col-
lart, who have all mastered the art of understanding how much psychology and ultimate profit lies
behind the so-called celebrity endorsement system.

Back in 1969, Colonel Obolensky organized a
three-day junket hosted by Mr. and Mrs. Jules
Stein (he is the chairman of the board of the
Music Corporation of America) to celebrate the
opening of the Sheraton-Universal Hotel combined with a benefit premiere of the motion picture *Sweet Charity*. Planes from New York and
Europe arrived in Los Angeles filled with their
own star-studded cast of characters.

From Europe there were people like Princess
Ira von Furstenburg and her father, Prince Tassilo
von Furstenburg; Duchess de Cadaval; Prince and
Princess Alfonso de Hohenlohe (he obviously
found the party such a good idea that he now
uses a similar technique in resorts like St. Moritz
and Gstaad, luring guests to a cocktail party that
is little more than a sales promotion for his Mar-
bella Club development). There was also Baron
Alexis de Rédé; H.S.H. Princess Gina of Liechten-
stein; Gaea Pallavicini; the David Metcalfes; Lady
Sarah Churchill and her Greek husband Theodor
Roubanis; Margaret, duchess of Argyll (she was
traveling light at that time with only eleven suitcases); the Portuguese trio of Patino, Schlumberger and Vinhas; and assorted others both with
and without titles.

The East Coast was represented by the Clyde Newhouses; Mrs. Albert D. Lasker; Mrs. Paul Felix Warburg, Susan and Gil Shiva, the Steins' daughter and son-in-law who acted as gracious hosts on the flight; Mr. and Mrs. Cleveland Amory; Louise Savitt; Francis Kellog; Mr. and Mrs. Oscar de la Renta; Charlotte Ford Niarchos and others.

Amidst all the gaiety at one of the parties, television commentator Rona Barrett was quoted as saying that "the Geritol Set was in abundance but the Pepsi Generation was conspicuously absent."

The *New York Times* attacked the trip as the "grossness in Los Angeles" in an economic period highlighted by reduced poverty programs, and mentioned that the House Ways and Means Committee might not look too kindly on the fact that tax money was being used to finance a three-day holiday for 600 jet-setters.

The press people and corporate heads were obviously not discouraged and the celebrity junket has continued to be used the world over.

For example, Liza Minnelli and a planeload of people were flown to Paris to introduce Love cosmetics at the Champs Elysées branch of Le Drugstore. In 1974 the Antenor Patinos flew Europeans and Americans to the gala opening of their Mexican resort development, Las Hadas in Manzanillo. The executives of Loew's International brought a planeful of guests, including Mary and John Lindsay, Ava Gardner, David Frost, designer Hanae Mori and others, to a party with Prince Rainier and Princess Grace celebrating the opening of the Loew's Monte Carlo in late 1975.

Until recently, one of the greatest patrons of those who want to live rich for next to nothing was Régine, the Queen of Clubs. She has two in Paris, three in Monte Carlo and one in New York, and has her sights set on Rio, Los Angeles and Houston. She puts all her nightclubs together with an unbeatable formula: Interior designer Alberto Pinto does the decoration, master chef Michel Guerard provides the artistic decoration of the cuisine, and the dancing is always done to superb music. The guests are always well dressed and glamorous—or they can't get through the front-door screening committee.

Take the preview of her New York club in Delmonico's Hotel in March 1976. For added punch there were music, balloons, dancers and more than 300 guests, plus an American debut of Régine's first dress collection, under the "Zoa" label. The prêt-à-danser" collection, as it is called, was filled with colorful, swinging chiffon dresses that look divine on her dance floors.

The $50-a-head benefit was to aid the Association of American Dance Companies, and dancers from the America's Second Century company modeled the dresses. Régine herself was dressed in one of her Zoa creations. Her makeup had been done by Jacques Clemente, her personal makeup man from the Paris branch of Elizabeth Arden, and her henna-colored coiffure had been poufed by Jean-Louis Hym of the Cinandre salon, the hairdresser who came to New York with Régine for her very first concert at Carnegie Hall, and stayed. Régine's husband, Roger Choukron, was busy organizing the waiters and staff to ensure that everything went off smoothly.

The guests exceeded the expected turnout and included Diana Vreeland, Diane von Furstenburg, Candice Bergen, Hubert de Givenchy, Pauline Trigère, Julio Tanjeloff, Christina Bellin, Jan Chipman and her sister, Buffy Cafritz, and Countess Marina de Brantes and Mrs. Marvin Traub, who were cochairpersons of the successful evening.

Looking around the Art Déco club and watching her guests on the glass dance floor, Régine commented to the *New York Times'* Angela Taylor: "The time is right for the club and the clothes." And the time is obviously right for Régine, too. She's come a long, long way from the days when she first came to New York for her concerts and the lavish parties hosted by Mica and Ahmet Ertegun of Atlantic Records, on whose label she records. These days, it is the rich and the famous who court Régine and hope that she will respond to their greetings with a first-name salutation.

Régine has absolutely no problem financing her ventures. There is a long line of wealthy backers ready to write their checks for her next club, her newest restaurant. In an era that is little known for gaiety, Régine is one international bright spot. Depressed London is still getting over its disappointment that she and Sir James Goldsmith, her local partner-to-be, have postponed the opening of a London branch of Régine's to cheer the English in their time of depression.

Of all the exponents of the art of living rich for next to nothing, one of the all-time greats must be writer Truman Capote. Earlier in his career Truman Capote gained increased fame and recognition for his award-winning book *In Cold Blood*. Following that, he became known for his superb humor and wit, constant good company and ever-growing list of famous friends who indulged him. In the late 1960s he reached the height of his fame and became the overnight party-giver of the year when he hosted his Black and White Ball in honor of his good friend *Washington Post* publisher Katherine Graham. The guest list read like the *Who's Who* of contemporary society and the party was talked about for months afterward.

Recently though, Mr. Capote, rather foolishly perhaps, bit the hands that have fed him. *Esquire* magazine ran several chapters from his forthcoming book, *Answered Prayers*, in which, after years of gossiping with the likes of Babe Paley, the Bouvier sisters, Lady Nancy Keith, Gloria Vanderbilt Cooper, he divulges all the nasty little confidences that have been shared with him on the banquettes of New York's best restaurants. If the howls of outrage created by just these chapters are anything to go by, then the publication of the whole book will create a big enough hoo-ha to drown even the Concorde.

Undoubtedly there are suddenly a lot of blank spaces in Mr. Capote's engagement book, but he probably took a calculated risk. The book may well make him rich enough to be able to afford the lifestyle he's been enjoying, free, for so long.

KEEPING UP APPEARANCES—THE PAST MASTER AND THE UP-AND-COMINGS

It may come as a shock to hear that Aristotle Onassis, whose name became synonymous with great wealth, was a sincere believer in the art of living successfully above your means—or, as he called it, "keeping up appearances."

In a revealing interview he gave in 1970 to a small Chicago magazine called *Success Unlimited*, Onassis listed ten rules for success, which were mainly a rather cynical prescription for appearing to be richer than you are. One of the rules was "Keep a tan in winter; to most people, sun is money." Another was "Live at a good address, even if you have to live in a room in the attic."

Of course Onassis was rich—you don't run a Lear jet and a 325-foot oceangoing yacht, as well as two Greek islands, on "appearances." But, as he warned his wife and daughter in his will, they cost real money to run annually—$150,000 for the airplane, $500,000 for the yacht, and around $500,000 for the two islands—and the supply of money isn't totally unlimited.

Although Onassis left his daughter assets worth in the region of $500 million—a $250,000 yearly allowance tax-free, plus the yacht, the islands and the apartments in New York, Paris and Greece— she will need to be a very shrewd businesswoman to maintain all those trappings of wealth. From the rather low profile she has managed to keep so far, it would seem that appearances don't matter as much to her as they did to her father, but then there are few people alive today who could ever try to emulate his flamboyance and style.

One of them, though, must surely be Adnan Mohammed Khashoggi, a Saudi Arabian business-man and financier who in less than ten years has put together an empire worth around $400 million and, if anything, has been more successful than Onassis in showing how effective a business ploy "keeping up appearances" can be.

His yacht, the *Mohamedia*, with its own hair-dressing salon, electric elevator and no less than ten separate safes and strong rooms, is moored either in Cannes or Monte Carlo. And his private Boeing 727, complete with $2 million worth of extras, like gold taps in the bathroom, has been featured in colorful, full-page splendor in *Fortune* magazine, where it could hardly have failed to be noticed by any businessman even idly thumbing through.

The way John Samuels lives would be way beyond the means of 99.99 percent of people in the world, but it isn't above his. At a time when most people with more than one home are selling off the extra ones and settling for one, Samuels has no less than six, four of which are convenient to his office.

One is a Fifth Avenue duplex overlooking Central Park, another is a Tudor town house in Forest Hills, next to the West Side Tennis Club. Most weekends he and his family are on their own private island in Long Island Sound, in a forty-three-room manor house that J. P. Morgan's heirs couldn't afford to keep up. For weekends when he doesn't go to the island, he has a retreat in Southampton, Long Island, built in the late 1920s by some of the Du Ponts and containing seventy-two rooms. When he's in Galveston he moves into the house he bought for his parents, which is considered the largest private dwelling in the town. Lastly there is the fashionable flat in the Albany, London's famous apartment house.

And things aren't bad at the office, either, where Samuels has a private office dining room and a French chef who formerly worked for Charles de Gaulle, not to mention a Turkish butler . . .

INHERITING STYLE, NOT MONEY

It's funny how you remember people. Harper Sibley and I grew up in the same town and knew each other casually. The only difference was that he had that great name, Sibley (that was also the name of the major department store in town), and mine, of course, was just plain Ackerman. Only three years my senior, Harper was at Groton and Princeton when I was at Ben Franklin High and Syracuse University, Everybody in Rochester thought that Harper Sibley was very rich, but he was not. What he had, though, was a great inherited name, lots of style and a good deal of brains.

The Sibley family has been prominent in Rochester and elsewhere for four generations. Harper's great-grandfather, Hiram, was a founder and the second president of Western Union. Another ancestor, Fletcher Harper, was a founder of Harper & Brothers, the publishing firm. Harper Sibley's father, F. Harper Sibley, was a gentleman farmer with extensive holdings in New York, Illinois, California and Alberta. A man who occupied himself with civic and religious activities, he was president of the United States Chamber of Commerce for two years, head of the USO during World War II, chairman of the International YMCA and president for thirteen years of the Church World Service, an international relief agency. He died in 1959.

Harper Sibley, Jr., is the youngest of six children and the only one who went into business in Rochester, New York. He did so without any family wealth but with those invisible assets of style, intelligence, drive and, of course, a great family name!

He started his career in 1949 after completing his education at Groton and Princeton, and though his first venture, with a real-estate brokerage firm, nearly ended in bankruptcy, he rebounded in 1953 with a 140-room Treadway Inn, built on land that had been in his family more than 100 years. The experience of arranging the financing for the motel prompted Harper, then twenty-seven, to start his own mortgage banking firm, which he built into the largest in upstate New York. The success of this privately held company, as well as of an insurance-brokerage firm he started, gave him capital to risk. He was a man who invested in ideas and concepts, not stocks in companies.

Through a series of deals, Sibley built up his capital base and his reputation. Then came the very big one—the Stirling Homex deal, in which he invested a mere $26,000 in 1968 and walked away, four years later, with a profit of about $12 million, a return of 46,000 percent on his original investment. After he and a group of his friends sold out, Stirling Homex Corporation went into bankruptcy in what has to be one of the great bust-outs of the 1970s. At one point the stock market bid the price of Homex shares to more than 200 times earnings, on the assumption that it really would become the largest company in a booming new industry. Since the fairy-tale success, Xerox, started in Rochester, many people were ready to believe that these upstate farmers were into another big winner. But the market was fooled, and in the end, it cost the company's shareholders and creditors more than $150 million.

At forty-nine, Harper Sibley is now enjoying life as the owner of a 3000-acre private resort in Key Largo, Florida—a business that lets him work in short sleeves, denims and moccasins. An affable and extremely likable person, Sibley comments bemusedly that his remarkable record for buying at the bottom and selling at the top was all a matter of luck.

Of course that's nonsense, but there is no question that Harper Sibley used all of his many talents to get ahead. Can you imagine how well he would have done had he inherited cash as well as a great name and style?

LIVING RICH OFF THE CORPORATION

The corporate world is only two or three generations old, yet already the man who controls the corporation—and who lives off it—is one of the most interesting twentieth-century phenomena.

Most of the executives who work for corporations—or own them—not only receive a salary, they also receive all sorts of bonuses, either in stock, cash or expenses. Whatever form they take, though, they all have the same effect: to give the employee a higher standard of living and, incidentally, increase his loyalty to the company, without including the Internal Revenue Service in the share-out!

If you are in a really big job, then you would expect the corporation to pick up the tab for medical care, club fees, transportation (company cars, for instance), household help, homes, travel, company legal counsel, accountants, facilities for entertaining, private recreation (golf courses, tennis-club memberships, swimming pools, gymnasiums, etc.), scholarship funds for children, dining rooms for executive use and various other fringe benefits limited only by a company's imagination.

By 1955 some 37 percent of all the Cadillac registrations in Manhattan and 20 percent in Philadelphia were in company names. A company dedicated to keeping its officers happy can, with

all propriety, justify a company airplane for business trips, a yacht and a hunting-fishing lodge or
vacation home. It can also arrange to hold its
conventions in Monaco, Paris, London or Rome,
although since the 1976 tax laws, you have to
be more careful and more companies are staying inside the U.S.A.

The effect, for company executives, is to provide wonderful vacations and travel, free! The
company officers can go south in the winter and
north in the summer, take along enough work to
justify the trip, and have it all paid for by the
company. At home they can also ride around in a
company-provided car with a company-provided
chauffeur, play in the best clubs and eat in the
finest restaurants. You name it and you can find
it among ordinary deductible business expenses.
Of course deductible expenses also include gifts
and other emoluments to oil the wheels of business friendships.

These are only some of the privileges of the
corporate rich on the dole, the legal and officially
sanctioned ones. You could argue that the ultimate in living rich on the corporation is the
presidency of the United States. In addition to
salary, the incumbent gets $50,000 a year tax-
free expenses, including the White House, the use
of planes, cars, boats, free travel, vacations and
many, many other extras—including an occasional spaniel puppy.

Still, looking at photographs taken of various
presidents after they've been in office a couple of
years and seeing the toll that the particularly
grueling nature of the job takes on them, you
might well wonder if it is actually worth it. Who
wants to spend his vacations in China, anyway?

For ordinary Americans, though, it has become increasingly clear that since the government picks up 50 percent of the cost of company expenses, one of the easiest ways of living rich today is by living on the corporation. In other countries, like Britain, expense-account living has become a thing of the past, but in America the corporation has become the anchor for wealth, and since you certainly won't be able to beat the system, you might as well join it.

Not too conspicuously, however. Recently the corporate people seem to have overstepped the bounds of keeping a low profile in these days of the Carter squeeze on government fringe benefits. The U.S. Securities and Exchange Commission and the Internal Revenue Service spotted a photograph in the *New York Times* sports pages of several corporate jets parked at the Augusta, Georgia, airport where the Masters Golf Tournament was being held. A story with the picture suggested that several of the planes were owned by major corporations.

As a result Mr. Stanley Sporkin, the enforcement chief of the SEC, was said to have remarked that company executives have been "using their companies as their own private piggy banks," and that from now on the SEC will pay closer attention to general and administrative expenses of companies to see if they deviate significantly from normal amounts. The SEC, he says, is going to rely on tips from corporate insiders and stockholders, as well as on reports from outside auditors.

A spokesman for the IRS believes that many corporate executives never consider that they may be using corporate resources improperly. "As people assume positions of authority, I think they don't always think of whether their actions are right or not," he says. "Who's going to question the corporate expenditure if he says 'Look, get the company plane ready. I want to go to Augusta.' "

While we think it is going to be tougher on the top men who really abuse the privilege, for most executives, living off the corporation has been and will continue to be a way of life. Who is going to decide what expenses are connected with business? Besides, for most companies the perks of corporate employment are a necessity if they are going to keep and motivate their key executives.

THE WORKING RICH WOMAN

There's a song in the old Broadway musical *Finian's Rainbow* that says, "When the idle poor become the idle rich, we'll never know just who is who or who is which."

Years ago the rich may have been idle, but today in many cases that's no longer true. The working poor, once they become rich, usually continue to work—the traveling is just as important and fulfilling as the arriving—and those who were born rich, and therefore had the benefit of the best education that money could buy, now want to make use of those qualifications and skills.

Years ago people also tended to assume that the more money you inherited, the less brain you had. (Playwright Samuel Beckett was once told that the pupils in his charge at a very exclusive, expensive private school in Dublin were the cream of Irish society. "Yes," he replied, "rich and thick!") That, too, is no longer true. Despite the image of bejeweled, empty-headed jet-setters, many rich people with active minds soon become bored with the endless social round of cocktail parties, lunch parties, dinner parties, and take jobs, not merely to fill in time but to give them real, personal fulfillment in achieving something with their own energy and creativity, not just with their checkbook.

As you'd expect, given that the working rich as a group have more self-confidence and style, better education and, very important, better contacts than most people, they have been universally successful in fields as diverse as politics, design, real estate and literature.

For some the motive for working is more complex. There are all the inherent problems of living in the shadow of an ultrasuccessful parent, or the identity problems of marrying money, or any one of a dozen reasons for feeling the need to improve themselves.

Take Princess Diane von Furstenburg, whom *Newsweek* called "the most marketable female in fashion since Coco Chanel" (March 22, 1976). The thirty-year-old princess by marriage parlayed her title, her savvy public relations image and her inborn merchandising instincts into a fashion empire that projects $60 million in retail sales this year.

Born in Brussels to a comfortable, middle-class Jewish family, Diane was a self-reliant young girl who was determined to get whatever she wanted. Her parents divorced when she was thirteen and she was sent off to finishing schools in Switzerland, Spain and England. While attending the University of Geneva, she worked briefly in 1965 for the then head of the Investors Overseas Services, Bernie Cornfeld, and subsequently met fel-

low student and future husband Prince Egon von
Furstenburg, whose mother, Clara Agnelli Nuvo-
letti, was one of the Fiat fortune heirs. Two years
later, despite his family's displeasure and the
criticism of friends, the couple married and Diane
became a princess. She recalls: "Everyone was
saying Egon was young, attractive, had a good
name and was rich. How could he be marrying
this Jewish girl who's absolutely nothing? I was
really hurt."

She may have been hurt, but Diane took her
revenge by marshaling her energy into creating a
career for herself. She apprenticed with an Italian
fabric manufacturer for a brief time and when
she moved to New York with her husband and
their first child she brought along three dresses
she'd designed using the Italian fabric. She
showed them to *Vogue*'s editor in chief Diana
Vreeland, who ran one of the dresses in *Vogue*
and started Diane on her career.

Meanwhile, Prince and Princess von Furstenburg were expecting their second child and fast
becoming the most publicized couple since
Amanda and Carter Burden. Despite the fact that
they seemed to have everything, the couple were
unhappy, and unpleasant rumors began to circu-
late about their marriage. But if the marriage was
deteriorating, Diane's career seemed to be thriv-
ing and she found herself with more orders
than she could fill. John Pomerantz of Leslie Fay
advised her to set up her own business and introduced her to Richard Conrad, an already successful entrepreneur who was looking for an investment and a company to run. He purchased 25
percent of the business and they opened up a
Seventh Avenue showroom together in the spring
of 1972. By 1973 the business had increased by

seven times and von Furstenburg came up with a winning wrap-design that proved flattering to every kind of female figure.

The marriage, meanwhile, had fallen apart and it even seemed that the playboy prince was jealous of his wife's success, for he tried to launch an Italian shirt line in America, which failed. Since then, he has moved back to Italy to continue his "idle rich" life among his idle rich peers; he spends much of his time traveling and has launched yet another menswear line.

As her business continues to be successful, Diane has expanded and put her signature on a wider range of products, including a line of cosmetics and a perfume, and has negotiated licensing arrangements to produce her furs, jewelry, handbags, scarves, shirts, shoes and sunglasses. A stunning and sensual brunette with a slim, sexy figure, von Furstenburg, like Estée Lauder, is her own best publicity. Her comings and goings are reported in all the gossip columns and her glamorous image is one with which millions of women identify when they purchase her products.

Her social life is hectic but she tries to limit her parties to those that count and she usually asks who else will be present before committing herself, "Otherwise, you can get stuck with the biggest bore, and I just don't have the energy for that anymore."

She and her two children live in a spacious Fifth Avenue cooperative (purchased with her own money) with an English nanny, an Argentine cook and assorted maids. Her weekends are often spent at the eighteenth-century farm she purchased as a birthday present to herself in New Milford, Connecticut, and during the summer she sometimes appears on Fire Island. There are critics who say that she, like Lee Radziwill, used her title to get where she is, but rival designer Halston defends her by saying that "her connections just make it easier."

Gloria Vanderbilt Cooper, on the other hand, was a poor little rich girl who had an underprivileged childhood in highly privileged settings. Her father died before she was two, and her mother, who was eighteen when Gloria was born, was never around. After a huge custody battle was fought over her, she ended up living with her aunt, her father's sister, who showed just as little interest in Gloria as her own mother had.

Now Gloria Vanderbilt has reversed the rags-to-riches story into riches-to-rags-and-back, hopefully, to more riches, with her successful collections of ready-to-wear fashions and a long string of design licensing agreements.

Although she never lacked material wealth, Gloria was not content merely to pursue the social butterfly role. Through four marriages, her greatest passion in life has been painting. She had her first show at the Bertha Schaefer Galleries in 1953 and since then has had at least twenty-five other exhibitions and three museum retrospectives.

From her paintings and collage work, she was inspired to do a collection of do-it-yourself collage kits. She also did puzzles and colorful paper products for Hallmark before going into fabric designs for Bloomcraft. From there she put her paintbrush to work doing sheets, towels and quilts for Martex; china, stemware and flatware for Sigma; table linens for Hallmark; bathroom accessories for Martin Garment's, eyeglasses for Zyloware and scarves for Glentex. In the works are projects for shoes, handbags, costume jewelry, cosmetics and a perfume called Gloria V.

In an interview in the weekly newspaper *W*, Gloria Vanderbilt said: "I am the most fortunate person in the world in that I get paid for doing something I love to do more than anything else." She said that she worked hard to get where she is and explained: "The story of my life is the song Billie Holiday used to sing: 'Mama may have and Papa may have, but God bless the child that's got his own.'"

When asked why she's so ambitious and compulsive about her work, the explanation she gives —that it feels good—is undoubtedly true for many of the other working rich. "Money that I make has a reality for me that other money doesn't really have."

Thirty-two-year-old Lally Weymouth, the Radcliffe-educated daughter of the *Washington Post*'s Katherine Graham, has just completed her second book, *America in 1876*, and she's ready to go on to the next project. Tall and slim and thoroughly attractive, she manages to balance her intellectual life with an active social life.

Divorced from architect Yann Weymouth, by whom she has two daughters, Lally lives in a smart-looking East Side apartment where she also works. She says that when she's writing she usually gets up at 7:30 and works at the typewriter until 11:30. After that, she might do some research at the library or pursue the active social life that has thus far gotten her more publicity than her writing.

The fact that she has two sides to her life makes her difficult for some people to understand. Her editor at Random House, Jason Epstein, explains that "most people think of Lally as a socialite who wears Halston dresses and flits around town. . . . She's a Mack truck, even if she does have a grand apartment."

OTHER WAYS OF LIVING RICH

Do You Really Need Your Own Airplane?

Most people associate travel with holidays, high spirits and success. For the rich, however, the antidote to imminent disaster seems to be to hop onto the next plane and get as many miles from the trouble as possible. There seems to be a direct correlation between the unhappiness of rich, famous people and how much traveling they do. Everyone who has ever prepared for and gone on a holiday knows how travel can take your mind off things like problems and miseries. Therefore, the very rich and famous, who seem to have more frequent and graver crises than the rest of us, are in a state of perpetual motion, never staying long enough in one place to have to face the problem at hand and actually do something about it. And if the suffering jet-setter is going to be airborne most of the time, what better way to travel is there than in a private plane?

If you haven't traveled by private jet, or so they used to tell us, then you just haven't traveled, and according to the 1976 sales figures—Gates Lear Jet sold 79 planes, Cessna Citation sold 69, Falcon sold 58, Sabre sold 28, Grumman II sold 18, and so on—there are still a lot of people traveling!

If you want to live rich, at some time you will probably consider the possibility of owning your own plane or investing in one for your corporation. Admittedly most private planes in the United States are owned by large corporations, but occasionally you'll find a nut who owns his own Lear jet. A nut like me. I was in good company though; I'm sure you've seen Arnold Palmer getting out of what looks very like a Lear jet to make it in time for the big tournament, and at one time the famous Boston lawyer F. Lee Bailey flew one too, though he seems to have traded it in recently for his own helicopter.

If you are seriously thinking of buying your own airplane, the best advice we can offer is: Forget it, unless you have so much money that the odd hundred thousand here or there makes no difference to anything. To be honest, a trip in your own private plane is the ultimate ego trip, though the rationalizations usually go along these lines: Time is money, and the best way you can save time is by having your own plane.

Not so. We have flown in almost all the corporate jets and everything else from a Cessna 150 right up to a Grumman II, and they all represent a terrible way to travel. Even with the bigger planes, range and speed are important considerations, and unless you're prepared to invest in a Grumman II at $3.5 million, none of them can even make it across the United States, and flying to Europe is more trouble than it's worth. In a Falcon, a Hawker Siddley DH 125, a Jetstar Dash 8, or a Lear Jet 25, you can add at least three hours to a scheduled airplane's flying time.

And then there's the cost. First, you have to buy the thing, and that can cost you between $500,000 and $1 million, *used.* A good second-hand 1971 Falcon, with 350 hours on the engine and 75 hours since the last overhaul, would cost you about $1 million. For a new one you can add another $500,000.

As for the operating costs, we've put together a realistic annual budget for a Falcon owned by a corporation and a Lear Jet 25 owned by one of those nuts we mentioned earlier:

> First, the pilots: around $55,000 for the two
>
> Next, the hangar and office rental: around $11,000 for the Falcon; $6,000 for the Lear jet
>
> Maintenance, repair, gas and oil: for the Falcon, $113,695; 25 percent less for the Lear jet
>
> The crews' living and traveling expenses: another $9000.
>
> Insurance: for the Falcon, around $27,000; for the Lear jet, $24,000

The total operating cost of the Falcon comes to around $218,448 a year, while the total operating cost of the Lear jet runs about $130,000 a year. With both the Lear jet and the Falcon, you might be able to knock between $25,000 and $40,000 off your operating costs if you get someone else to operate the plane for you and rent it out when you're not using it, but that depends partly on luck and partly on the personality of your pilot.

When considering costs, you have to remember inflation also. A year's operation of the Lear Jet 25 back in the early 1970s cost us around $116,000. Now it would cost at least $150,000, and if you add to that the cost of borrowing the money at around ½ percent over prime rate, you can see just how expensive it really is.

But in spite of all that, you might still argue that the expense is worth it for the convenience of having a plane to take you where you want to go whenever you want to go there. Again, not so. With a medium-size jet, no matter how good your maintenance, you'll find it's under repair or overhaul around 20 percent of the time—inevitably when you want to use it most. You'll probably find that after a one-way trip from New York to Los Angeles the plane needs maintenance, so you'll have to leave it and its pilots in sunny California while you try to get a seat on a commercial flight back to New York.

Don't be misled into thinking that it's the "jet" part of the airplane that causes all these hassles and that you'll be all right if you go in for a solid, old-fashioned "prop" model. It's true that a prop plane is cheaper. A used King Air will set you back around $500,000, a small new Merlin IIA around $320,000, or there's always the slower Queen Air at about $155,000. But all these airplanes have one thing in common: They are slow, noisy and cramped, and they are all a waste of time and money.

If you need something to get you into hard-to-get-at places or small airfields, then rent, don't buy. That way someone else has the headaches of ownership, and the premium you're supposed to be paying for renting, not owning, turns out to be the best discount you can get! The airplane salesman will tell you about wonderful resale values and how little your airplane will depreciate, but don't be taken in. No one we know has ever made money out of investing in an airplane.

Here's an example of just how inconvenient and annoying it can be when you have your own Lear 25 at your disposal.

One winter not too long ago we decided to fly out to Alta, Utah, for a week's skiing followed by a week's sunshine in Acapulco. As usual we were late making our reservations at the always crowded Alta Lodge and the owner, Bill Levitt, not only had to find us a double room but also had to squeeze in our pilot and the copilot. This accomplished, we set off from Butler Aviation at LaGuardia Airport on a cold December day, for Alta.

On the way, of course, we had to set down in Grand Isle, Nebraska, for refueling, but the necessary stop wasn't too annoying because the two women who operate the internationally famous Midwest refueling stop are renowned for their homemade brownies and rum balls, which they dispense to everyone who uses their landing strip.

We arrived in Salt Lake City perhaps an hour or so behind the time it would have taken to go commercially and the four of us (including pilot and copilot) loaded our luggage into a taxi for the drive up to the resort in the Wasatch Mountains. The next morning we were up early to begin our skiing and, over breakfast, we shared a horrible thought: Suppose one of the pilots broke a leg. With that in mind, we set off looking for a ski instructor for the copilot who was a novice skier and we decided to ski with the pilot in order to keep an eye on him.

The week in Alta was a delight and we had few problems before setting off for Acapulco, where we had rented a beautiful three-bedroom condominium on the bay, complete with two Mexican maids and a swimming pool. At the Acapulco airport we tried to rent two cars—one for us and one for the pilots—but, as it was the Christmas–New Year holiday, cars were scarce and we were only able to get one. Not wanting to deprive the pilots of a car, we set off to one of the local hotels, where we were able to rent a car that belonged to the assistant manager, who was pleased to give up the use of his car for the black-market rate he charged us.

The situation at the apartment was very comfortable and, aside from the fact that the two non–English-speaking maids couldn't understand how one woman could divide her time among three men (they kept urging, "Rest!"), we were having a good time.

Departure day arrived and we left for the airport in 93-degree weather, only to find out that for the Mexicans it was still siesta time and no one would charge the battery of any private aircraft until 4 P.M. Obtaining this bit of information took a couple of runs up and down the airfield tarmac, where the temperature must have been at least ten degrees higher than in town. At four o'clock we stood in line behind the commercial flights, and finally got our battery charged by 5:30 P.M.

Our first stop was New Orleans for refueling and a Customs check, but when we got there the Customs men were all out on coffee breaks and refused to come back to check a private plane. Their excuse was that if you're flying private, you can wait. We sat around the Customs office for over an hour, and when they finally arrived they turned our bags inside out. ("If you're flying private, you're rich and you probably bought tons of stuff in Mexico.")

When we finally arrived at Butler Aviation—twelve hours after leaving the apartment in Mexico!—the car and chauffeur who had come to meet us had long since given up on our ever arriving and had left. At that point we decided that it was a helluva lot easier to travel commercial. We told the pilot that we never wanted to see him again until he had found a buyer for the Lear 25, and off we went hitching a ride into town with our skis slung over our shoulders and carting our suitcases.

A Life on the Ocean Waves

Like many successful men before you, you may well decide that the only real escape from the pressures around you is to get away from it all by investing in a boat.

Before you do, though, there are three important factors to bear in mind. First, that buying a boat does not mean simply buying a boat. You also need, if you want to avoid that irksome drive to the marina, a waterfront house with its own dock, or, at least, a condominium in Florida or California, unless you're prepared to rough it by actually living on the boat.

Second, the only boat worth having is a "yacht" —which means either a small private ocean liner, like Bill Levitt's *La Belle Simone* and the late Aristotle Onassis's *Christina*, or a really high-powered ocean racer, built for speed, not for comfort. As some wit once said, ocean racing is rather like standing under a cold shower, tearing up $100 bills.

Which brings us to the third factor—the cost. With yachts, the maintenance costs increase geometrically, not to say exponentially, with the length and the "beam" (width), and they can be a veritable Pandora's box when it comes to hidden costs, as a yacht-owning friend of ours—let's call him Bob for the sake of the story—discovered.

Having acquired significant wealth through the sale of his company to the public, when such things were still possible, Bob decided to buy a modest boat—fourteen feet long, with a twenty-four-horsepower engine. To avoid the thirty-minute journey to the marina, he decided to rebuild the time-ravaged 300-foot dock at his home, which, by the time he'd paid for new pilings, decking, dredging and installing electricity and water, cost him about $40,000—all to service $2800 worth of boat!

And his problems were only just beginning. His family complained about the toilet facilities—a bucket in the cockpit somehow lacked style—and about the way the boat rolled unmercifully at low speeds and threatened to dislodge their kidneys at high speeds. Eventually they got to Bob, so he decided to sell her, but not before she'd sunk twice, which involved not only rebuilding the engines but some rather terse discussions with the insurance company about negligence.

Remembering his days as a summer-camp sailor on a small New Hampshire lake, he decided to buy a sailboat, considerably larger than the first boat, to silence all the family's complaints about lack of comfort and seaworthiness. Since he was planning a round-the-world trip anyway, he stopped off in Hong Kong and, after some days' deliberation at the shipyards there, settled on a thirty-five-foot sloop with teak decks and interior, a "head" (toilet), shower, sleeping accommodations, a tiny galley (kitchen) and even a steering wheel. To save on duty, he bought the boat without engine and sails. He wanted an American diesel engine anyway, not the British one the boatyard fitted as standard, and he'd also heard about the alleged poor quality of mechanical workmanship in Hong Kong.

The boat finally arrived by sea and road at a Long Island boatyard, and Bob waited impatiently for the fitting-out to be finished. Suddenly, engines were unobtainable. And, he was told, the boat hadn't been built properly.

After several months the boat was delivered. The workmanship—other than the Chinese—was atrocious, and whatever he'd saved on duty he'd lost many times over in the delays and poor quality of the finishing. The boat, completed in Hong Kong, would have cost Bob around $22,000. Completed in Long Island, it cost him nearer $30,000.

And then, after all the hassles, the boat turned out to be too spartan for Bob's taste. Worse, it lacked style and the aura of success that is as important a feature to any boat owner as the sails or spars. What he *really* wanted, he decided, was something larger, racier. In fact, something he could enter in the Bermuda Race—after all, more than one captain of industry has hit the sportspage headlines in that free-for-all!

Although other thirty-five-foot, ready-made yachts had successfully made the run, Bob would be satisfied with nothing less than a forty-six-foot, custom-built yacht from the drawing board of one of the top designers. Not only would she be fast, the designer reassured him, she would be roomy enough for anyone, except perhaps an oil-rich sheik with a string of wives.

When finally the yacht was ready for sea trials, the costs were almost *double* the designer's original estimates. As he'd promised, she was fast, and beautiful, but the accommodation was nowhere near adequate for those idyllic Caribbean cruises that Bob had been planning. True, he had the private double cabin aft that he had wanted, but at the expense of the "head." As it was, only a man under five feet tall could urinate standing up, unless his backbone was as flexible as Nureyev's. Since the only time Bob ever intended to kneel aboard his boat was on Sundays or during a Force Ten gale, he put her on the market right after her maiden voyage.

A man not easily discouraged, Bob then began to hunt in earnest for his ideal craft. He found her on the Miami River—a sixty-foot, German-built yacht of the highest standards of comfort and quality. Having paid a "reasonable" six-figure sum for her, Bob had her taken to the shipyard and gave orders for her to be ready for a cruise to Bimini and Nassau in three weeks' time and "to hell with the expense." The shipyard carried out his orders—the work was completed on time and the bill was staggering.

With scarcely a tremor, Bob paid it, provisioned the yacht and, with guests and crew aboard, set sail for Bimini. The skipper took to his bunk almost the instant they left port, leaving Bob as navigator, engineer and captain!

Later, there was the new engine Bob had to fit *and* the diesel generator *and* the new radar *and* the new single-band radio. . . . Skippers came and went—five in one year—and each one had different ideas about what equipment the boat *had* to have. One skipper even obliged Bob to send a technician from New York for the sole purpose of showing him how to start the generator. Tools, supplies and fittings seemed to disappear without explanation. Generator failures often left the yacht without cooking facilities, so Bob and his friends either had to eat ashore or borrow from passing yachts.

Then, to cap it all, Bob found that the pressure of work meant he could only get away for a maximum of five weeks each year, and it suddenly occurred to him to work out how much each of those five weeks' yachting cost him. The answer was a staggering $10,000 to $15,000—over $50,000 a year!

Bob may have been a yachting "nut," but the economics rapidly made him recover his sanity. The boat was put up for sale, and though it was a bad time for selling anything in the luxury market, a buyer eventually appeared.

Bob admits that his five years' boating cost him over $350,000.

Anyone for tennis?

Anybody for a Haircut?

A great haircut is not merely one of life's great pleasures for any man on a spending spree, it is also an investment—it can make you look thinner, younger, more elegant. What's the point of spending $300 on a suit if your hair looks as though it was cut by a well-trained dog?

There are certain barbers throughout the world who can do the right job for certain men, and their loyal clients will travel the width of the United States, or even the Atlantic, rather than let another barber near their hair. For years, Philip at the Beverly Hills Hotel barbershop was the man for me. He could cut my hair in a way that made me look ten pounds slimmer. Almost anytime I was there I saw luminaries of the business world getting trimmed and shaved, whether they lived in New York or London. The barbers in that shop actually had an international reputation. In New York, places like Paul Molé, Jerry's at Bergdorf's, all have customers who would rather grow their hair to Tiny Tim lengths than get a haircut anywhere else.

Once you find a good barber, stick to him. He is probably—in terms of value for money spent—your best investment. Indeed, like any really good investment, you'll always find a businessman shrewd enough to put his money where his hair is.

For years, David de Rothschild was a client of Desfosses, a staid, all-male hairdressing salon on the Avenue Matignon, patronized by brokers, bankers, businessmen, even politicians, including the French president, Valery Giscard d'Estaing, who walks in regularly, usually on the eve of one of his televised chats, for a trim.

When David de Rothschild heard that Desfosses was closing down because of financial difficulties, rather than face the hassle of having to find a new barber, he decided to buy the place. He did not simply take it over; he put together what you might call a conglomerate in male chic by bringing in as partners Michael and Maurice Renoma, his favorite tailors. They had started out with a small shop in Montmartre twelve years earlier but, due largely to the success of their *style minet* (best translated as "young" and "in" though it certainly loses something in the translation), they had later opened a shop in The White House in the chic 16th arrondissement, one of the most elegant menswear stores in Paris.

The new salon, renamed Desfosses-Renoma (Desfosse himself retired, leaving the use of his name), is a 700-square-meter complex spread on two floors. It has been cleverly revamped by Michael Boyer, who has worked with a blend of sober, masculine tones—dark gray, beige, black and a dash of rust for the suede settees. The chairs are not those up-you-go, down-you-go and around-you-go barbershop jobs. Instead, they are like huge, black leather thrones with a vibrating massage system built into them. The lights have a flattering pink sheen, and there is a bar, a secretarial service, a sauna, a pedicure room—even a room with a sign on the door reading, unashamedly, *Sains de Beauté* (Beauty Treatments).

Actually, this story is more of an enticement for the barber, when he sees to what heights he can aspire.

Are Diamonds a Girl's Best Friend?

It has been said that diamonds are a girl's best friend, and maybe they are, but it all depends on who bought them. If you get them for nothing as a gift, then they represent a very good investment. The best investment is always one that has value but no cost. On the other hand, if you plan to buy precious gems as a substitute for fixed interest securities, our best advice is, Don't.

Like many other investments of this kind, unless you plan to make a careful study of the market, know the prices at which precious gems sell and be prepared to hold them for a long time, then you probably should not be in this kind of market.

While you don't have to be a millionaire to invest in the very-best-quality precious gems, such as diamonds, rubies, sapphires and emeralds, you must have enough capital to understand that this kind of investment has a very low liquidity level, and you must have sufficient other capital to be able to hold on because there is a large difference between the buying level (retail) and the selling level (wholesale). For most people, there is no way to buy at wholesale level, as even the auction houses of Christie's & Co. or Sotheby, Parke,

Bernet Inc. are, in reality, retail operations, and to buy wholesale you must be a well-established diamond merchant in good standing with the DeBeers operation in South Africa.

While you can buy a very high grade one karat diamond for $6000 to $7000 retail, a gemstone-quality ruby for $6000 and a similar 1 karat emerald for $7000 to $8000, buying gems is a tricky business. Retail markups on fine-quality gemstones are usually 30 to 50 percent, and with bigger gems you can usually bargain but the markup is still around 20 percent.

As investment, you then have to wait at least five years before you can even consider selling, and then, unless you have a really good, reliable jeweler who will handle the stones for you, your only out is the auctions, where prices tend to be much lower, selling commissions are high, and only the really superb-quality gemstones fetch high prices. In addition, you will have to consider the cost of insurance, if you can get it, and the fact that you or the woman who wears them might get held up or even killed by a burglar who decides to take them.

Aside from investment, jewelry has other uses. Some men we know often buy their wives important pieces of jewelry to ease their own guilt feelings. The greater the infidelity or attachment to the current girlfriend, the more expensive the bauble that he brings home from a so-called business trip. The gift of a jewel is supposed to reassure the wife that he loves her. Then there are other men who buy their wives large, expensive pieces of jewelry and insist that they wear them whenever possible in order to impress their friends with their success. More than once these gifts have proved useful later on when the men were strapped for capital and needed collateral for loans. Twenty percent interest and possession of the diamonds, rubies, emeralds and sapphires are paid to certain jewelers, but when business picks up, the jewelry is always redeemable.

The Cigar—Supreme Happiness

The cigar, like the haircut, the hairdresser, cosmetics and clothes, is for many people an essential for supreme happiness. As time passes and one becomes more aware of the few little pleasures in life, a good cigar begins to represent the ultimate in living rich. For me, smoking a cigar is the ultimate in relaxation and peace of mind.

The other day, when we went to pick up our monthly order of cigars from our London tobacconist, J. Fox and Co., Ltd., we had a little chat about the rising prices and varying quality of Havana cigars. According to Mr. Fox, the proprietor, the quality of the Havana cigars has fallen while the prices have increased over 50 percent in each of the last three years.

One of the great pleasures of living in Europe is that you can smoke the finest Cuban cigars whenever you want—provided, of course, that you can afford them. When it comes to choosing a cigar, the "cabinet selection" are always the best. These cigars are packed in large boxes without cellophane and seem to have a much firmer texture. Once you have selected the brand you prefer, the next consideration is one of size, which is often determined by what you feel most comfortable holding and smoking. Of course the occasion should also influence the size—for after-dinner smoking you need a firmer, larger cigar than you would for smoking during the day.

If you are a guest in someone's home and the host offers a choice of cigars, by all means ask his advice. Chances are, if he has been thoughtful enough to provide a choice, he will be able to describe the condition of his cigars and may even suggest a sort of smoking program for the evening: perhaps a light-colored cigar of medium length first, a Colorado; a darker and larger one, such as a Demi-Corona, after dinner. Never smoke a light Havana after having smoked one that is stronger—that's a lesson I've learned from experience.

My education in the art of cigar smoking has improved since I came to live in London. I've learned, for instance, that a cigar that is smoked more than halfway down extinguishes itself rapidly when you stop drawing on it because the concentration of tars dampens the fire. It is a sad moment and bitter to the taste, but it is the point beyond which it would be uncivilized to try and prolong the cigar's life.

Also, be careful with the remains of your cigar. I always get rid of them as quickly as possible to avoid agitating my hostess and to avoid the odor of a "cold" cigar. By all means let the cigar die by itself—don't crunch it out in the ashtray and hide the remains. At home, I have my own small silent butler to keep my remains out of sight and smell. My wife, however, has discovered a new use for the remains. Rather than simply throwing them in the trash can, she boils them in water and sprays our windowbox plantings with the solution once a month to kill any lice that tend to gather in damp London. The nicotine is instant death to the aphids—which makes my wife wonder what it's doing to me.

If you have friends who smoke, or you yourself smoke, you know that men who like a cigar will go to any length to get Havanas into the United States—in spite of the fact that their importation is against the U.S. Customs laws. One man we know has a Swiss bank account solely for the purpose of paying his Zurich cigar dealer to send his Havana cigars into the country disguised as Dutch cigars. Another favorite trick of some cigar stores is to remove all Havana labels for delivery to the United States and replace them with Jamaican ones.

Thousands of illegal Cuban cigars enter the United States annually in various guises. Foreigners can bring them into the country, supposedly for their own consumption; traveling Europeans become favorite dinner guests when they bring their host a bread-and-butter gift of a box— or even a handful—of fine Havana cigars.

What the United States needs is a cigar-smoking president with enough guts to lift the embargo. There must be several thousand votes out there from would-be Havana-cigar smokers who would rejoice at being able to smoke their favorite cigars legally!

Polo—at $6000, a Bargain?

Polo isn't exactly a growth sport in the United States, or anywhere else, and its survival, if only as a pastime of the very rich and very elegant, amounts to a triumph of tradition and "style" over almost insurmountable practical difficulties.

Invented by the ancient Persians, polo has been the sport of the rich and indolent since the nineteenth century. To play it, you must be not only extremely skillful and a first-class horseman, but also extremely rich. A good polo pony (they're called "ponies" but they are in fact horses) can cost you $4500 or more, and of course one pony is no good to you—you need a string. Then, depending on the number of ponies you have, whether or not you employ your own trainer and how much traveling you do (if you're a serious competitor, you do have to travel since there are only 140 registered clubs in the United States, not to mention internationals), your total annual costs could be in the region of $25,000.

You can do it for less, of course—$6000 can get you started, if you buy two ponies at $800 each, a two-horse trailer for $2100, plus a minimum of $500 of tack and equipment. If you keep the ponies at home, then feeding them, at $3 a day, would cost you $1095, veterinarian and blacksmith fees would be around $250, and club dues around $500—a total of about $6045.

And what do you get in return for your investment? The rewards are largely intangible: a pride in good horsemanship, the singing crack of a mallet against a willow-root ball. But as every salesman knows, rubbing shoulders on a sports field with potential customers can never be bad for business. Start playing polo and you could find yourself playing with—or against—Robert Uihlein, Jr., the chairman of Joseph Schlitz Brewing Company; or William T. Yluisaker, chairman of Gould; or John T. Oxley, an independent oilman; or Paul Butler of Butler Aviation, who has been largely responsible for keeping the game alive in the United States.

Your Own Gym
More and more, people who live rich are vulnerable to ailments that may relate to lack of exer-

cise—mental fatigue and high blood pressure, heart disease and so on.

To head off these disasters, why not build your own gymnasium, for you and your friends? A modest gym at home can be set up for about $2000, excluding the cost of an instructor. You could have a variety of machines, including an Exercycle and a treadmill for jogging in place. You could also spend up to $75,000, if you want paddle tennis, an elaborately equipped exercise room, sauna, showers, lockers and a place to relax and watch the big football games on Sundays.

TO LIVE RICH YOU MUST BE AN INVESTOR

There are two kinds of people in the world— spenders and savers. The spenders, no matter how much they earn or inherit or acquire, never seem to have enough, and the cost of their pleasures, whether it's wine and food, travel, buying paintings, gambling or philanthropy, always seems to exceed their available resources. The savers, on the other hand, no matter how small their income, are always prepared to postpone their enjoyment and use the money instead to make more money.

If you want to live rich, then there are three courses of action open to you. You can cross your fingers and hope you win a state lottery, or play the Good Samaritan to an elderly stranger you come across, in the hope that he may turn out to be another Howard Hughes and leave you around $160 million in his will. Or you can learn to invest.

Chances are that unbeknown to you, you are already an investor. If you have an insurance policy or belong to some kind of pension and

profit-sharing scheme, then you are already part
of America's investment structure. Pension funds,
insurance companies, even banks, are all investors on a big-scale. In fact in the last ten years the
"institutional investors" have virtually dominated
the stock market.

You might think that there is safety in numbers
and that in something as potentially risky as investment the big financial institutions probably
know best. Not so. Time and again it has been
shown that the small individual investor can do
better for himself by going it alone than by hand-
ing over his investment funds to an institution
(though that is not to say that all collective investments are automatically bad, but more of that
later).

Once you have decided to become an investor,
there are almost limitless possibilities open to you.
Companies of all shapes and sizes are almost always in need of investors' money. So is government, at both the local and national level. There
are innumerable books and articles on the subject,
but what we are going to do in this book is concentrate on the areas of investment that you don't
usually hear about—your own house, for instance,
or art, and those investments made by the financial institutions who need that little bit extra in
the way of interest so they can pay you your
interest on your investment with *them*, and make
themselves a profit at the same time!

We sent a friend, author Patrick O'Higgins, to
his bank, Morgan Guaranty Trust Company of
New York, to inquire about buying some Eurodollars at a time when the interest rate was
around 11½ percent for a twelve-month deposit.
All he got was double-talk and he became so discouraged that he wound up with domestic certifi-

cates of deposit, paying a rate of interest at least three points lower.

Why did they talk him out of it? Because that, after all, is how they make their profit, and how can they hope to make money if you invest your money as well as they do?

The banks may not like it, but what we aim to do is show you how you can make that extra percentage or two on your money, which will give you that extra bit to spend, or to reinvest, or at the very least to help you keep pace with inflation.

There is no magic formula for success in investment, but you should be aware of three main points. First, you must be aware of what you hope to accomplish. Second, you must have a knowledge of the subject—when, where, how. And third, you must have a real determination to succeed, and not to let yourself be discouraged.

In the following chapter we will show you whole areas of investment that you may not have known about before, and help you understand the risks involved. It really isn't difficult—all it takes is common sense, the will to succeed and a little courage!

5

INVESTMENTS

RISK-TAKING

The basic fact about any investment is that the rewards are commensurate with the risk: The greater the risk, the greater the rewards, and vice versa. Practically every investment that tries to limit the risk involved also reduces the potential reward. So, whether you plan to invest your money in the stock market or the commodities market, in modern art or Roman coins, in a Broadway musical or longhorn steers, the first question you must ask yourself is: How much risk am I prepared to accept?

The answer will depend in part on how much capital you have and what your philosophy of living is. Do you need the income from any investment to "live rich" or can you opt for a long-term capital appreciation with no income during the months, even years, it takes for your investment to mature?

If you do need steady and safe income, there is no merit at all in investing in art, or in a bond offering 15 percent interest, because the risk that you might never receive a penny of that 15 percent is just too great.

Think very carefully about liquidity, too. If you need cash to pay back a short-term bank loan, you cannot invest your money on a long-term basis. More investors have gone broke that way—bor-

rowing "short" and investing "long"—than almost
any other. It was one of the main reasons for the
recent real estate investment trust fiasco. It's
probably the toughest game of all, and unless
you're a real pro with nerves of steel and enough
resources to survive a heavy fall, avoid it at all
costs.

Investing in anything other than commercial
bank deposits, certificates of deposit or Eurodollar deposits—all of which guarantee your cash
from the investments—as a major or sole source
of investment is a bad idea if there's any chance
that you'll need instant liquidity. Suppose in 1971
you had put all your money into shares on the
American stock market, or into paintings or even
fine wine, and four years later, when you needed
the cash, decided to cash in your investment. You
would have soon made the painful discovery that,
following the stock-market crisis and the virtual
collapse of the art market and the fine-wine
markets, it was almost impossible to find a buyer
for what you had to sell, unless you were prepared
to take a good deal less than it was worth, and
almost certainly less than you had paid for it. In
the spring of 1976, at Sotheby, Parke, Bernet,
several impressionist paintings—one of the hottest
"safe" art investments four or five years ago—
failed to reach their reserve prices!

If you can afford to ride out a slump in the
market and wait until it picks up again, then your
Chagall gouache will probably pay you better dividends in the long run than having your money in
thirty-day certificates of deposit at the Chase
Manhattan Bank. But if you can't afford to wait,
and *have* to sell, then you will lose money, and
any investment that actually loses you money is
obviously a bad investment.

When you're deciding how to invest, you should also consider what you need the money for. If the investment is for your children or your grand-children, then you might consider a very different investment from one you might make if you needed the money to finance your life-style.

If one of the most important factors in deter-mining how you invest is risk, then you'll need to consider also the most important factor in deter-mining how great that risk will be—the workings of the economy. A careful reading of the daily newspapers and the odd specialist journal should give you a reasonably good grasp of how the econ-omy is likely to go. It's true that nobody foresaw the oil crisis in 1973, which made a tremendous difference to everyone's investment strategy— governments' as well as individuals'—but on the whole, the financial writers do a pretty good job of charting the economy's future course. At least you can get a feel about market values, com-panies' earnings and interest rates. If, like Ber-nard Baruch and Billy Rose, you can outguess the experts, you might be able to make not merely an investment but a killing. On a more realistic plane, though, just being able to see whether the market is going up or down, when the turnaround is likely to come and, especially, to anticipate changes in interest rates should give you some in-sight into how the workings of the economy will affect your proposed investments.

Having decided exactly how great, or small, a risk you are prepared to take with your invest-ments, your next step is to learn how to maxi-mize your investment within those limits.

Take, for example, Charles Bluhdorn's com-pany, Gulf + Western. In 1975 the company borrowed dollars *outside* the United States and issued Eurodollar bonds. (More of Eurodollar investments later; briefly, they are a type of international bond, denominated in any currency and usually sold outside the country whose currency is being used. They are a major source of investment, not only for banks, institutions and foreign investors but for ordinary American individuals, though at the moment a relatively unknown one.)

Gulf + Western's Eurodollar bonds sold in 1975 were brought to the market with an interest coupon of 9¾ percent, while Gulf + Western bonds on the U.S. stock market were yielding at least a point less. For all practical purposes it is the same company and the element of risk involved is identical. Therefore, knowing about the Eurobond market and how to invest in it means that if you want to invest in Gulf + Western you can get more for your money, with no increase in risk.

Clearly, unless you understand what risk-taking is all about, you won't get very far with your investment. Worse still, you could lose everything before you've had a real chance to get started.

THE FUNNY INVESTOR
WHO LOST MONEY IN THE MARKET

Stanley Marsh III, 38, "the funny investor" according to a recent article in *Forbes*, wears bizarre clothes, sits in his office under neon sculpture and is "crazy" like a fox where his investments are concerned.

For all his flamboyance, no one underestimates Stanley Marsh. "Stanley thinks in his sleep," vows one Texan who was on the losing end of a business battle with Marsh. And he's successful. He has made a killing in small business investment corporations and banks. His Amarillo TV station, a money-loser when he bought it, now prospers with the highest Nielsens (60 percent) of any ABC television station in the United States in a three-signal market. Marsh concedes his reputation for eccentricity may close some doors to him, but not many. "Intelligent people will treat you intelligently or not deal with you at all, regardless of your style."

Marsh makes some of his investments for fun as well as profit. He cornered the market in Israeli bar mitzvah commemorative coins "because I wanted a legal monopoly." He put money into a far-out solar-energy-insulation scheme because he's interested in the technology. Marsh's mother wanted to back the jet-set designer Halston just for the glamour of it when he set out on his own after doing hats for Bergdorf Goodman. The investment proved a gusher when Halston sold out to Norton Simon, Inc. Marsh's falling in love (with the girl from the ranch next door) also proved serendipitous—the bride brought a cattle fortune into the family fold.

There is method behind most of Marsh's madness. Explaining why one of his chief aides is a Marxist historian, Marsh says: "A Marxist understands capitalism in a different way from a Milton Friedman. I want to know all the rules of the game so I can win."

One investment area where Marsh admits to being a loser is the stock market. "Instead of buying stocks, I bought 'hot' brokers," he says. Marsh dropped a bundle. Now he keeps just enough money in stocks to backstop his frivolity—in case it turns out that he's the most incredibly naïve fool that ever walked the earth in making all the other investments. It's not likely he'll need the backup.

THE STOCK MARKET

Advice on how to invest in the stock market could well be responsible for the world paper shortage. There are literally thousands of books on the suject and also, of course, the *New York Times*, the *Wall Street Journal*, *Business Week*, *Forbes*, *Dun's Review*, to name but a few, which will tell you all you need to know about the basics of investing.

The Psychology of the Market
If you're going to invest in the stock market, you should also understand the market psychology. Less obvious than major external economic events but equally important is what we self-styled psychologists call the behavior of the crowd, or the herd instinct.

There is an old market proverb, "Buy on the rumors, sell on the news," and like most old proverbs it contains a half truth. If a company is booming, or about to collapse, then the insiders who have close dealings with the company—the employees and the analysts who follow a company's fortunes—will know the facts long before they are published, no matter what the Securities and Exchange rules tell us. As the market waits for the hard facts about any developments, informed rumors will be spreading and both buyers and sellers will be acting on the *expectation* of what is about to happen rather than waiting until it actually does.

Thus stock prices will rise or fall on the rumors, not the news, and if you, as an inexperienced investor, are not in tune with the rumor market and have to make your decisions based upon the published news, you will always be too late. If you yourself can predict an event—a loss that nobody knows about or a chairman losing his job—then you are ahead of the market, not behind it. Since the market puts a price on tomorrow, not today, you must be ahead of the pack or you don't even have a fighting chance.

The tendency is for the crowd all to be pushing in the same direction at once. As a smart individual investor, you will not simply let yourself be carried along by the tide but will ask yourself if you are moving in the right direction, if your broker knows what's really happening, or if you are being used. A healthy skepticism about everything you are told is the best defense against the enthusiasm or pessimism of the market. Understand why the advice is given and ask yourself if it is the best for you. Remember, exaggeration is the keystone of investing in the stock market.

Back in the early 1960s we tried to make money trading stocks and we lost a good deal. For every winner that our broker gave us, he gave us ten losers. Many of our friends used to say, like Stanley Marsh III, invest in a good broker, not in a good stock. But try as we might, we never found a broker who didn't have his own interests at heart instead of his customers'. That is not to say that stockbrokers are any more dishonest than the next guy, only that a good broker who works for his customers is hard to find. If you find one, stay

with him, for he is a rare commodity. Otherwise,
if you really want to trade stocks, you must be a
broker yourself or own your own seat on the stock
exchange, or you are playing a fool's game.

In short, we believe you cannot make money
by trading stocks. That is a business for professional market men, not for the ordinary investor.
It's best to forget the temptation and all of those
phony stories you hear about making big money
by trading in the market. No one ever talks about
the stocks on which they lost money.

Hand in hand with this market psychology goes
the philosophy of cutting your losses. "Your first
loss is your best loss" is another old market proverb, which happens to be true, although attaining
such philosophical detachment is no easy task.
Try to keep clearly in mind your reasons for investing. You buy shares because you expect them
to increase in value and make you some money.
If the opposite happens and their value drops,
then take a calm, realistic look at the situation
and try to understand why. Obviously we are not
talking about the normal ups-and-downs of the
market; we are talking about a stock whose value
has fallen. If that is the case, then no matter how
right the decision to buy it may have seemed at
the time, you have made a mistake. Perhaps the
most important lesson you can learn is how to
admit that you were wrong, to cut your losses
quickly and get out.

Far more money has been lost by people refus-
ing to cut their losses than by people who cut their
losses early and move on to the next investment.
It is tempting to hang on for "just a few more
days," or weeks, even years, like a modern Mr.
Micawber, waiting for the market to "turn up." If

you do, you could wind up losing 50 percent of your investment, maybe more, whereas is you realize your mistake early and get out, you may lose only 10 or 15 percent. People who make money on the market are those who are prepared to cut their losses. Those who aren't—the optimists who hang on and on and on hoping for better times—are the big losers.

Timing is everything, and if it's true that what goes up must come down, then the moment to get out is near the top or the moment the graph takes a serious downward turn. A stock that falls heavily takes a long time to recover, and many never recover at all. You'll make more money ultimately by taking a small loss and reinvesting in something new than in leaving the money where it is and just waiting.

In the case of a company going bankrupt and liquidating, the order in which investors are paid off is: bonds first, then preferred stock, then common stock. Keep that in mind.

Learn by your mistakes, but don't worry about them. There really is no profit in crying over split stocks.

Understanding the Terms

We are assuming, of course, that if you are interested in investments you already have a working knowledge of the terms of the trade, as follows:

1. *Equities*. Shares of stock in a company, bank or other entity selling on the market are called "equities." In effect, the shareholders, of which you become one, own the equity in the corporation or that which remains "after the rights of creditors of all kinds." The equity in your pri-

vate house is the market value less the amount of the mortgage. The equity in a company or bank or other entity is the value of the assets remaining after the creditors have been paid what they are entitled to receive.

2. *Dividends.* Unlike fixed-interest investments, the very nature of an equity is that dividends are declared, not fixed. The indicated yield from an equity is the income at the latest dividend rate, calculated by reference to the market value at the time of purchase. Obviously no investor can know at what rate a dividend will be declared in the future. That is the big difference between equities and fixed-interest securities;

3. *Earnings.* As a shareholder you are theoretically entitled to your share of any profits of the company that remain after all prior claims have been satisfied. This includes the money retained for growth and those profits paid out as dividends. At this point it starts getting complicated, but if you understand "dividend cover" and "price/earnings ratio," you know enough.

The "dividend cover" is arrived at by dividing the amount of the dividend which *could* be paid from the year's earnings by the actual dividends paid. Thus, where the dividends paid represent one-third of the available earnings, the dividend is said to be covered three times.

The price/earnings ratio, the be-all and end-all of investment analysis, may be defined as the number of times the price of the equity capital on the market can be divided by the earnings available. Alternatively, it is the number of years it would take the company to earn the present price of the shares, assuming no change in the earnings. So, in a company with earnings of $500,000 a year after tax, and one million shares of stock at the price of $5 a share, earnings would be 50¢ per share, with the stock selling at ten times after-taxes earnings.

4. *Book value.*   The value of the earnings and assets of a company, after prior claims have been satisfied, is termed the "book value." This information is supposedly found in the balance sheet, but beware. The assets should not be assumed to be worth the values placed on them in the balance sheet. The real book value may be more or less than the balance-sheet figures, and varies in different circumstances.

Unless you are looking at the company with a view to running it yourself, or you think the company may be in financial trouble, the market book value is less important to you, as an investor in the stock, than earnings. But some of the best values in the market today relate to understanding book value, especially with the trend toward cash offers for undervalued companies. A stock selling at 50 percent of the company's book value can turn out to be an excellent investment, if it looks like a candidate for a take-over and the acquiring company is prepared to offer a premium over "book" on the cash tender offer.

Several of the professional funds play this game all the time. With a low price/earnings ratio, and a discount from "book," the stock may very well have a low downside risk, but a great upside potential if it is a candidate for a takeover.

With the market cooling off again, the spirit for movement is returning with the takeover specialists back looking for interesting candidates.

Diversification
Diversification is the name of the game—sometimes.

The market operates in cycles, and under normal circumstances it is not a good idea to place all your eggs in one investment basket. But if you are convinced that you have a really good strategy, then back your judgment and risk a lot of money in one stock rather than a little in a dozen different stocks. Here's an example, based on personal experience.

Reading in the newspapers and magazines about the New York City crisis, you could not have failed to see how the commercial banks in America were under terrific attack, and, for the most part, justifiably. The banks had overloaned in several dangerous areas—for example, in real estate through the REITs. Coping with the recession, the banks had also taken a hard knock with the collapse of the Franklin National Bank and Security National Bank in New York, and United States National Bank in California. Other, smaller banks were in danger of collapsing, but, even so, the system wasn't under any real strain. The banks of America are probably the most regulated and conservative industry in the world. Without the banks, the American system could not even begin to function, and, in our opinion, there was no way the federal or state governments would let them collapse.

Our conclusion that the banks were going to survive—in spite of the REITs, the New York City failures and the fact that some banks had gone into liquidation—was the basis of an idea for an investment strategy in the market. We called up our stockbroker and asked to see information on the major banks, recommendations from the brokers and other sources like trust departments at banks, and so on. The information we got is shown in Table 4.

Bank	4th Qtr. 1975 $ Mil.	Chg. From 1974 %	12 Mo. 1975 $ Mil.	Chg. From 1974 %	P/E 2-27	12 Mos. Earnings Per Share
Alabama Bancorporation	4.4	2	17.5	12	7	3.14
American Fletcher	2.3	−42	12.6	−11	6	2.75
BanCal Tri-State	−1.2	NM	3.3	−50	15	0.94
BancOhio	6.0	−4	24.0	6	5	3.29
Bank of New York	8.0	−23	33.4	−2	6	5.56
Bank of Virginia	3.2	14	11.4	7	6	2.50
BankAmerica	82.8	10	301.7	18	11	4.37
Bankers Trust New York	12.3	−41	63.8	−11	6	5.88
Barnett Banks of Florida	2.0	1	11.4	−35	9	1.34
Charter New York	9.5	−7	45.1	12	5	5.14
Chase Manhattan	19.2	−69	156.6	−14	6	4.89
Chemical New York	22.4	−17	98.6	7	5	6.83
Citicorp	73.5	−9	348.2	11	11	2.81
Citizens & Southern Natl. Bank	3.2	NM	15.8	61	12	0.55
Continental Illinois	30.1	−24	119.0	−17	7	6.85
Detroitbank	7.2	−3	28.0	7	5	8.78

General opinion was divided; some thought bank stocks were cheap, others thought that they were not cheap enough.

At this point we made up our own minds and decided to invest in bank stock. But which ones? The yields were high, anything from 7½ percent to 9½ percent, and the price/earnings ratio very low. To all the information we had gathered, we added our own experience in dealing with banks over the last fifteen years. Some, we decided like Chase Manhattan, were not well run; others, like Chemical Bank, were very well run. Besides, Chemical had made a superb acquisition in the assets of Security National Bank, the Long Island bank that had gone into liquidation. Once the Security assets were cleaned up, the Long Island network of branches that Chemical acquired virtually for nothing would provide a great "plus" for earnings in the future, since we knew Long Island and we dealt with Security under the old management. We also knew that the Chemical losses, while potentially quite large, could be shared by the government in tax credits, and that Chemical has the potential to increase its capital without too much strain.

While some of the other bank stocks also looked good, we finally chose just this one. What made us decide on Chemical was the fact that we have used them for years as one of our banks and they always seemed to know what they were doing. There is no substitute in the market for an inside view of how a company—or in this case a bank—operates.

To digress for a moment, it was also an inside view of both Franklin National and Security National, as long as six years ago, that warned us that both banks were doomed. At the time, we controlled a small bank in Beverly Hills, the Republic National Bank and Trust Company of California, which used to buy participations in other banks' loans, among them Franklin National and Security National. From a portfolio of many millions of dollars' worth of loans, the local bank examiners singled these two out, as a result of their published facts, as being destined for financial trouble. Even though we had the right to "put" these participations back to these two banks at any time, the examiners gave us notice to get rid of all our participations with them.

At first, we were indignant because we knew the management of these banks and, after all, they were two of the larger banks in the New York City area. But after a long session with the local examiners, we were convinced that they were right and we were wrong. Sure enough, five years later both banks were in liquidation. It's too bad that the New York examiners were not as astute as their associates in California; they could have saved the banking community a lot of headaches.

Time and again we have found that an approach to investment based on personal knowledge and experience is the soundest. That's why we chose Chemical Bank for an investment in late 1975, at the height of the New York City crisis. We bought heavily the one stock, in the one industry, because we thought we understood that particular situation the best. We didn't diversify: We bought against the market and the psychology of doom. We made this investment because it met our primary criteria:

(a) The stock yielded 9.3 percent—a good rate at the time and probably secure, even with the losses.

(b) We were investing in something we thought we knew about: what constitutes good management in a bank.

(c) The risk of losing our capital was minimal because banks hold a key position in the American economy.

(d) This particular investment had fair liquidity and we could get out quickly if we believed the fundamentals of the situation were about to change.

(e) We invested on a nonborrowed basis, so that we didn't have to worry about margin requirements or loss against the stock.

(f) Long-term, we saw upside potential with recovery of the market and a better position for banks generally; but, more important, when we combined the yield and the quality of the stock, the risk seemed minimal.

That is what we mean by understanding a market investment, not just investing in the market. So against the trend were we that although we tried to persuade several friends and relatives to follow our strategy, none of them were interested; they thought all the banks were going broke, or at least the ones in New York City.

Meanwhile the stock, bought at around $29 a share, near the low during the middle of the New York City crisis, has risen to approximately $39 per share. Of course, we cashed out near its high of $42.

Stocks as a Hedge Against Inflation

Until 1973 most financial advisers advocated the purchase of equities in growing companies as the best hedge against inflation for the average man. The market was always going up, and the possibility of it ever coming down seemed as likely as rain falling upward.

But after the stock market of 1973, the oil crisis, the subsequent recession, and the threatened bankruptcy of New York City, most people who followed that advice are wondering what went wrong. In a few short years it had become transparently, not to say painfully, clear that a down-market could wipe out all the profit and much of the capital, with only a few brokerage fees to show for all that effort.

As you know, it is our belief that investing in the market was bad advice before 1973 and is probably even worse now, especially in the light of the new market in 1978. And for most investors, merely buying shares, putting them away and forgetting about them is the worst advice of all. All the evidence about averages for the last five years indicates that investing in shares is not as good as just leaving your money in a 5½-percent savings account which guarantees you, at least, the principal and interest on a safe basis. Table 5 illustrates just how well common stocks did compared with fixed-interest securities over the last five, ten and fifty years.

Many a pension-fund trustee is waking up to this fact, but, frankly, he has only himself to blame. There is no question that the securities industry has the best of public relations and "Invest in America" is the greatest single slogan since "Invest in Liberty Bonds." Furthermore, by invest-

TABLE 5
1926–75
Market Indexes and Inflation

	5 yrs. 1971–75	10 yrs. 1966–75	50 yrs. 1926–75
Inflation (Consumer P.I.)	6.8%	5.7%	2.3%
Treasury Bills	5.7	5.6	2.3
Quality Corporate Bonds	6.0	3.6	3.8
Common Stocks	3.2	3.3	9.0

SOURCE: Data on inflation, treasury bills, common stocks and high-quality corporate bonds are rates of return from a study entitled *Stocks, Bonds, Bills and Inflation: Year-by-Year Historical Returns,* by Roger G. Ibbotson and Rex A. Sinquefield.

ing in the stock market, the securities industry claimed you could expect your shares of stock to provide, through increasing dividend income and capital growth, a return that was more than sufficient to compensate for the decreasing purchasing power of your money.

That has proven to be a pipe dream. In *The Bulletin*, Frank K. Reilly, on "Companies and Common Stocks as Inflation Hedges," says:

> In an economy where investors apparently do not anticipate inflation, one can only expect common stocks to be an inflation hedge if companies in general are able to hedge against inflation. Unfortunately the several generally accepted means which firms can use to hedge against inflation are not possessed by most corporations, or the benefits are short-run. As a consequence one should not expect common stocks to be inflation

hedges except during unusual economic periods such as 1950 when corporations were apparently able to be superior inflation hedges. The empirical results for common stocks confirmed this expectation.

The foregoing does not mean that stocks will never be an inflation hedge or that some individual stocks could not be an inflation hedge. The theory and empirical evidence does indicate that investors should not expect common stocks in general to be inflation hedges. More realistically, one should expect to have to conduct an extensive analysis of the relevant variables to find prime candidates.*

The fact of the matter is that if you want to invest in the market you must realistically seek out candidates through extensive analysis, companies that do meet the specific requirements of an inflation hedge. Such a search is beyond the scope of this book. We can only urge you to obtain good, professional advice from somebody who really knows his subject, not from the great bulk of brokers or trust departments who grind out their recommendations either to sell stock or to keep you happy.

However, even those who have employed the services of professional money managers over the last ten years may well ask whether the fees have been worth it. A recent study shows that bank and insurance-company commingled funds and mu-

* Frank K. Reilly, "Companies as Inflation Hedges," Bulletin #1975-2 of the Center for the Study of Financial Institutions of the Graduate School of Business Administration of New York University. Copyright © 1975 by New York University.

tual funds as well have failed to keep pace with inflation. In fact, the situation is much worse than that. A. S. Hansen, Inc., an actuarial consulting firm in Chicago, has just completed a survey of 161 banks and 45 insurance companies and has found that, for the decade ended December 31, 1975, leading market indicators have done better than the average fund managed by professionals —and by a substantial degree.

Again, we can only say that we have not found advice from brokers or trust departments to be competent, unbiased and free from self-interest. Therefore we make our own decisions and focus on the things we personally know about.

For example, one of us was brought up in Rochester, New York, and worked with the Eastman Kodak Company for a number of years, and we believe that this is the kind of stock, in spite of its low current price, which you could bet on as an inflation hedge. First, the products—photography and chemicals—will grow with the population. But more important is the quality of the management, though this isn't something you can discover from the company's balance sheet, or the analysis of profit and loss. Only from personal business experience is it possible to distinguish those companies in which management has been exceptional.

The quality of a company's management is the key to a long-term investment strategy and it is by far the most difficult factor to assess and evaluate. It is the most dominant influence, nevertheless, on the price of the company's stock. Management's ability to recognize changing circumstances, and to amend policy to take account of those changes, is the principal growth factor in the success of the best companies. Make a list of those companies you know something about on the major stock exchanges and evaluate them from your own experience. Don't downgrade your own opinions; they could be as good as, or better than, your broker's.

Backing your own judgment is as good a means as any of reaching a decision about which stock to buy. It's certainly better than taking your tips from the license plates of automobiles (spotting EK97 means that if Eastman Kodak stock is currently around $80, it's a good buy, as Everall Mattlin suggested in his *Status* magazine article, "Keeping Up with the Dow Joneses,") or from the size of the crowd looking in the window of your nearest brokerage house!

Use your common sense. Look at the company's product; did you buy it in preference to any of its rivals? If you did, chances are lots of other people do, too. Your opinion here is as valid as any stockbroker's. Diane says her experience with Originala is a case in point, and she tells the following story:

> While I was working on a magazine in New York, I covered a number of fashion shows—among them, Originala, a firm celebrated for its high-priced, high-fashion, superbly cut coats. After the show, which was a great success, I learned from the president that they were planning to expand into a younger, lower-priced range of coats.
>
> I knew that it was a small company with not too many shares of stock outstanding, that their standards of quality control were very high and that obviously they had the

formula for fashion success. By the time I got back to the office, I had decided to buy some Originala stock. I checked the listing in the newspaper, saw they were on the American Stock Exchange and rang my broker with an order. He asked why I was buying Originala, and when I gave him my reasons he thought I was crazy. Most women, he said, go to fashion shows to buy new coats or dresses, not stock!

At that time the stock was selling at $16 a share. Six months later it was $32, and my broker rang me to ask if I'd been to any good fashion shows lately.

Remember, the market price reflects the view of investors—and that means you as well as the professionals—as to the further potential of a company and, obviously, its share price. Get the technical facts from others, but rely in the last analysis on your own opinion. Surely your own experience can help in picking out the well from the poorly managed companies. Maybe it's the one you work for now, or have come in contact with over the years, as we had with Chemical Bank and Originala. You have as much chance of being right, if you study the situation, as the professional investors.

The Special Situation

If you have the extra cash and can afford the risk, find one or two young companies, companies that have gone public within the last five years. Examine the management, the product, and the market psychology behind the stock—for example, who sponsors the stock in the market?—and ask yourself, Is it a promotion or the real thing? The stock will probably be selling on the over-the-counter market but it may be on the American Stock Exchange.

Only after you've looked at the company with critical eyes, as if it were your own company, should you make your investment. Look at the necessary time scale. Do you think it will take five years or ten years to make good, or is it just around the corner, one or two years away? In either case, don't use short-term funds and don't expect a quick return. This kind of investment is always a long-term situation if it makes any sense at all. If it's an "in-and-out" then it's a promotion and you will never, or seldom ever, get out before the professional promoter. His investment view is different from yours and there is no way, in the long run, that you will come out ahead in an "in-and-out" situation. You may hit it lucky the first time, but be assured that you will lose on the next few because the odds are similar to gambling. The smart winner in Las Vegas walks away after the lucky win; the real gamblers put it all back and the house always wins. Just look at the profit figures from the big Las Vegas casinos before assuming that you can break the bank.

If you have inside knowledge of any companies that fall into this "special situation" category, so much the better. Perhaps a relative or a friend is on the board or works for the company in a key executive position and can give you some insight. Remember, however, that theirs will be "special interest" advice and you'll need to filter out enthusiasm and self-interest from hard facts or else you could really be taken for a ride. You're only human and you'll *want* to believe that you are getting privileged information, but it's possible that you are only being used to "hype" the stock, to spread the good news. Therefore, study inside tips very carefully.

If the tip comes from a professional stockbroker, then forget it. By the time a "hot tip" reaches you, it's old news and not even worth a phone call. Good brokers don't deal in tips but in facts, and though tips can affect a stock, in the end it's facts that matter. As an example of how tips—rumors—can affect a stock, Diane recounts her experience in appearing before the grand jury.

Back in 1972, Martin was acting as attorney for Clifford Irving, who was in the middle of writing what everybody—Howard Hughes excepted—believed to be Hughes' autobiography. For a couple of months, Cliff lived with us and the house took on the appearance of a huge press room and journalists' cafeteria combined.

After the *real* story of Clifford Irving's trips to Mexico came to light, both Martin and I were called before the United States Grand Jury. During my ninety minutes on the stand, I was asked by the U.S. attorney if I had ever had any financial dealings with Clifford Irving. I replied that I had. Just before he moved in with us, I had met the president of a company called AG-MET, INC., which specialized in recycling X-ray material to extract the silver. We'd met on an airplane and I had been so impressed by what he told me that I phoned my broker just as soon as we touched down, and ordered a quantity of the stock, which was then selling at $4 a share. I told

Cliff about the company. He caught my enthusiasm and decided to buy some of my shares, and wrote me a check, there and then, which I returned to him uncashed when the whole Hughes hoax came to light.

The U.S. attorney asked what had happened to the shares, and I told him that they were now selling at $11 a share. He then turned to the Grand Jury and asked if any members had any questions for me. One man raised his hand and asked if I would please repeat the name of the stock. As I spelled it out, A-G-M-E-T, I saw forty pens or pencils appear and forty heads bend over, as they all wrote it down. Within two weeks, accelerated buying had pushed the price up to around $14 a share. Draw your own conclusions!

As it turned out, in this special situation the tip was a worthwhile one. With hindsight, we sold too soon, not because we didn't have faith in the company but because we had already made a profit and you never lose money by taking your profit. Greed can spell doom when you invest in the market.

New Issues

New stock issues fall into two main categories: those of existing public companies seeking simply to raise some additional capital, and those of companies going public for the first time.

With the former, whether or not you buy the new issue depends on the same criteria that applied to the stock before the new issue, and indeed to almost any other stock on the market.

With new issues from new companies, a totally different set of criteria apply. Admittedly, many of today's household names started as small businesses many years ago and people who bought their new issues did very well. Equally, a number of small, unknown companies today will be the household names of tomorrow. In general, however, most new-company issues are a waste of time, since the motive behind the move is either tax considerations or, more likely these days, the raising of capital, and it's unlikely that you will make money.

The 1960s was the boom period for new issues. Without exception, they seemed to increase in value straight after the public offering, so not only were the brokers only too keen to take companies public, but the investors were more than happy to hand over their money. In the long run, though, the only people who made money out of the new-issues market were the brokers. It was not so much a market as a promotion—a situation to be avoided like the plague unless you have real inside information.

During the slump of the early 1970s, brokers were much less eager to take companies public. Now, with the market beginning to pick up again, there is no doubt that that particular bandwagon will start to roll again. That is not to say, though, that every new company's new issue is automatically a bad investment. If a successful and expanding company decides to go public, if a prominent stockbroker or firm is prepared to act as underwriter, and if the financial conditions of the company meet with your investment criteria, then it might be a good investment.

Always bear in mind, however, that brokers are

fundamentally salesmen and that they earn their living selling stock to people, so don't be taken in by the sales patter. If in doubt, wait; you can always buy the stock after it has been introduced onto the market. It will cost a little more, but if it's a good stock, all that means is that you'll make a slightly lower profit. It it's a bad stock, then its price will already have begun to fall and you will have saved your money.

In the final analysis, it's better to miss out on a good stock—there are always plenty more where that came from—than to saddle yourself with a bad one.

Selling Short

You will no doubt hear a lot of people telling you to "sell short." Don't—unless you really need ulcers and maybe a coronary, and you enjoy throwing money away.

Selling short is a gamble—you are betting that the market is wrong—and what it involves is selling stock you don't actually own. Suppose stock in Schmuck, Inc., is selling at $100 a share and you are convinced that it is so overpriced that its value must come down soon. You call your broker and ask him, virtually to borrow a hundred Schmuck shares on your behalf, for which you put up either cash or stock as collateral. You then sell those shares at the current up-tick market price, $100 each. If your gamble pays off and the value of the stock begins to fall, you wait until it reaches, say, $50 a share, and buy a hundred shares to replace those that you borrowed. Having sold at $100 and bought at $50, you'll have made a very neat profit of $50 a share.

It sounds easy, but it isn't. If the market is

right and you are wrong—the value of the shares goes up and up instead of down—you could lose your shirt! It's probably the riskiest investment game around, certainly not one for amateurs, or for most professionals either, unless they have nerves of steel and are prepared to back their conviction by hanging on.

Back in the early 1960s, when I was starting out and willing to try anything—once, at least—I tried my hand at selling short. A small company I had worked with and knew pretty well, Pioneer Parachute Company, had just gone public and its stock had reached a price which I thought was impossible to maintain, even on a short-term basis. Neither the management nor the broker handling the stock was involved in any promotion, and as nobody could suggest any substantial reason for the stock being so highly priced, it seemed inevitable that it would soon come down. It appeared a perfect candidate for selling short, so I bought in on that basis.

Unknown to me, however, the company had been working on a revolutionary new parachute which floated rather than fell—or something like that. *Life* magazine got hold of the story and splashed it across five pages, so that the stock—which had obviously never heard of the laws of gravity—soared up and up and up.

My nerve cracked—I decided to cut my losses and get out. Eventually the price did start to come down and had I hung on I wouldn't have lost so much money, but I'd have been a basket case and in no fit state to enjoy the money I would have saved.

Our advice: Stay away from short selling unless you have a very, very special situation.

Letter Stock

Letter stock is another game to be avoided by everyone but the real pro. Letter stock basically is unregistered stock often issued by small new companies to avoid the cost of formal underwriting. It is usually offered for sale by your friendly neighborhood stockbroker/promoter.

Generally, the major disadvantage with letter stock is that it cannot be sold for at least two years, and then only under Rule 144 of the Securities Act of 1934, which imposes severe restrictions. What happens, in effect, when you buy letter stock is that you become a very junior partner in the company and, unless you and your friends hold enough stock between you to have a real say in the running of the company, all you have is very-junior-partner's rights—that is, none.

That's not to say millions and millions of dollars have not been made in letter stock. They have; but generally, as an individual, you will not be invited into a few good moneymaking deals around, and most of the other letter-stock deals are out-and-out promotions, to be avoided like the plague.

If, however, you're approached by a firm like Allen & Co., one of the best in the field, or by one of the bank trust departments, then it's certainly worth taking a close look at the deal they're offering. Before you go ahead, you must understand that you'll be sacrificing liquidity in a letter-stock deal, but it may be worth it if the senior partners are good, reliable and, more important, have invested some of their own money.

We just invested about $4000 in such a situation, but, here, 60 percent of the deal is owned by a major bank and 40 percent by a group of sophisticated investors. The 40 percent is on invitation and could have been sold many times over. We have looked at the company carefully and we think it can make it big, but basically the decision was made because of the caliber of our partners. We think they are smart, and there is more capital where the original came from if needed. The time scale we see in this investment is between five and ten years and we know that we are locked in for a long period of time, with no yield on investment for at least three years. But then again, so are our partners.

If you can find such deals, and have the extra cash, then by all means consider them. The hardest part here is to get the invitation, not make the investment.

Investment in Your Own Company

From what we have said, it becomes quite obvious that the more you know, the better your chances of coming out ahead in the stock market. Therefore, it makes the most sense to invest in yourself. Whether you are the major stockholder, a key employee, or have an opportunity to obtain options in the company you work for, investing in your own stock is good advice. On balance, most of the people who have made it really big have made it because they believed in themselves as their own best investment.

That still holds true today. If you are employed by a public company, then persuade your management that employees who own stock in the company have a greater interest in their jobs and turn in better performance. There is no better incentive than spreading the company's wealth among its employees.

Perhaps one of the most important decisions I made with my first major public company was to set up a stock-purchase plan and to try to persuade as many employees as I could to take up their shares. The plan provided for stock purchase over a ten-year period at around $8.50 a share, with interest charged at a nominal rate. Many homes in Arizona, Seattle, Charlotte and Philadelphia, not to mention cars, swimming pools, the children's educations and all the other essentials for living rich, came from the profits of that plan.

A surprising number of employees were not interested, however, and one key man turned down most of his allocation, a decision he came to regret bitterly since most employees sold their shares for anything between $9 and $88—the highest price reached during those bullish days in the 1960s.

Options
The option game is another way of playing the stockmarket game; it's a way of buying stock for smaller sums than the direct purchase of the same shares would require. An option is the right to buy or sell a share at a particular price, usually over a period of up to three months. The purchaser pays only for the option, either a "call" option, which gives him the right to buy the option, or a "put" option, which gives him the right to sell during the option period. Alternatively, he can acquire a double option, which entitles him to either buy or sell.

The cost of the option may be two or three points higher than the price of the shares, and because of the additional cost of the option, price movements in a given stock must be quite large

for the options to be worth anything. For this
reason, dealing in options is certainly more speculative than dealing in shares. Many options that
are bought are never exercised, and therefore the
cost of the option is lost.

Our advice: Stay away from this market, unless
you intend to become a professional market operator, close to market information and able to keep
an eye on the trends of the market. However, in
your own company or in very special situations,
the option is quite worthwhile because it gives you
a chance to invest for a smaller outlay. If you are
interested, we are sure that you can find a great
deal of good information on the option market.
Be careful, and remember the risk: You invest a
lot less money, but the chance of losing it is
greater.

Buying on Margin
According to the New York Stock Exchange,
"Every new margin account owner discovers a
new world. And he is often pleasantly surprised
to find that margin investing is by no means as
complicated as he may have been led to believe.
However, if he is properly informed, he will also
realize that the greater opportunities available to
him through margin's added purchasing power
can be offset by greater risk of capital loss than
is involved in strictly cash investing."*

You may notice that the New York Stock Exchange doesn't say anything about borrowing, but
that's what margin is all about. In the normal
case, you would buy your stock and then send it

* Reprinted with permission from *Margin*, published by
the New York Stock Exchange, Inc. Copyright © New
York Stock Exchange, Inc., 1976, 1977.

to your bank where they would be delighted to give you a loan against the stock of some 5 to 80 percent of its value, depending upon the quality of the issue. The rate would be about ½ to 1 percent above prime, and you would be required to add to your account if the price of the stock fell below a certain level.

In using a broker's margin account, in which you only have to put up a percentage of the purchase price of the stock and your broker advances you the balance, you achieve the same results, except that the rate is higher; your broker has to borrow the money he is lending you from the bank, so on top of the bank's interest rate, he adds his own overhead and profit. The risk is also greater; at your broker's, the rules are laid down by the Federal Reserve Board and "margin calls" (demands for more money if the value of the stock falls) are strictly regulated, whereas at your bank the rules are less rigid and you are less likely to be called on to increase your margin.

The advantage of "margining" is that you don't have to find the whole cost of the stock before you can buy. Your broker likes it too, because, in theory, it leaves you with more cash available for further stock purchases, which means more commissions for him. It's riskier, however, because you don't have the whole amount, even as a reserve, to cover the cost of your purchase and could find yourself in trouble if the value dropped sharply. According to the New York Stock Exchange, that most bullish of institutions, "Margin isn't the sure path to riches. It certainly is not the vehicle for the investor who is not prepared to face the possibility of severe losses in the marketplace."

Since all securities differ in value and personality, the Federal Reserve places varied requirements on different kinds of securities, as indeed do individual brokers and firms. Margin men have a formula: Add two zeros and divide by 65 (or 50, 25 or 15) to arrive at the dollar amounts you can buy with the cash you have available for margin investment under present regulations.

The Federal Reserve Board's current initial margin requirement, at the time of writing, is 50 percent. The required cash or securities must be deposited with your broker within five business days after the purchase in order to conform to federal law (Regulation T). Penalties may be imposed on both you and your broker if more credit is extended for the purpose of purchasing or carrying securities than the federal regulations permit.

Member firms of the New York Stock Exchange are also guided by the Exchange's minimum initial equity requirement of a cash deposit of no less than $2000 or its equivalent in securities. When you deposit securities instead of cash, the amount of credit that brokers allow is based on the value of such securities and, of course, the current margin requirement.

All brokers hold stocks purchased on margin in "street name"* and credit you with all dividends received on them. You may direct your broker how to vote your stock in proxy matters and sell your shares at any time.

You should realize, though, that it is almost impossible to make a profit on small margin pur-

---

* To facilitate trading, each financial institution buys stock in the name of a fictitious person, usually a variation of the company's own name, such as Mr. Banco.

chases. Commissions on odd-lot purchases—less than 100 shares—plus the odd-lot differential of 12½¢ per share, plus the loan interest, can equal or even exceed appreciation plus dividend payments.

And finally, the most dangerous risk you run in using margin purchases is the margin call. Your broker tries to keep your margin account from getting seriously out of hand, but, with the way the market operates, if the stock falls he will almost inevitably have to make a margin call on you for more money or collateral.

A Five-Point Checklist for Investing in the Market

Remember, investing in the market is something entirely different from investing in cash. To help you decide whether investing in the stock market is for you, consider the following:

1. Do I need my money for short-term commitments? (If the answer is yes, stay out of the market.)

2. Do I need to be guaranteed the income from the dividends? (If the answer is yes, then invest only in high-quality companies where the dividend is assured on a practical basis.)

3. Is the company in which I am interested in investing well managed, in an industry that looks like it has potential, and where growth is a significant factor? (Don't buy the company's stock if you have any doubts at all.)

4. How long am I willing to wait for my investment to mature? (If less than five years, it's not an investment but a speculation.)

5. Should it be stocks, or something else?

INVESTING IN BONDS

Though the stock market and the bond market
have a lot in common, stocks and bonds do differ.
The main difference is that with the former, you
are buying equity—a piece of the action—while
with the latter you are buying an "obligation"—
in other words, loaning the company money at a
fixed rate of interest. If the company goes into
liquidation, they are obliged to repay you before
the stockholders get their money.

There are two main types of bonds: *senior
bonds* and *subordinated bonds*. Senior bonds, as
their name suggests are first in line behind the
banks and other creditors in case of liquidation
and ahead of the stockholders and the subordinated lenders. Subordinated bonds give the holder
the right to convert into stock at a given price
and at a given time, still yield a fixed interest and
are still ahead of the stockholders in case of liquidation, but behind the senior bonds.

In most cases, trustees are appointed to protect
your interests as a bondholder, but, in fact, if the
company runs into financial trouble, they are
powerless to help you. Don't be lulled into a false
sense of security just because the notepaper lists
a big-name bank as one of the company's trustees.
That's just window dressing.

As a prospective investor in the bond market,
you will be faced with a bewildering choice of
available bonds, but, remember, there are a number of factors common to all of them. Almost all
carry a fixed rate of interest, payable either quarterly, biannually or yearly. The yield is higher
than bank deposits, commercial paper or other
cash investments because the market believes the
risk is higher; unlike bank deposits, there is al-

ways a chance that you won't get your money. All interest earned is taxable, and, like stocks, bonds are subject to capital-gains tax.

As with stocks, market factors like the standing of the company and the state of the economy affect the price of bonds, which, in turn, affects the yield. The higher yield of one bond against another means that the market believes that the bond with the higher yield has a greater element of risk.

In our opinion, bonds issued by sound companies offer a better investment, as a fixed-interest security, than do many of the investments in financial institutions like savings or commercial banks. Whether they are better than stocks is a matter of opinion. In the last two years they were a better investment; some experts say that stock prices will move to a premium over bond prices in line with the premium they have enjoyed over the last fifty years.

Yields are as much as 3 to 4 percent higher in the bond market than in the money market or the commercial banks or savings banks. In assessing the comparative quality of the investment in bonds, you should take into account the amount of other debt ranking in priority to the bond offered, the earnings of the company available to meet the interest, and the security offered by the financial soundness of the company in question.

In recent years the convertible fixed-interest security has become extremely popular. The right to convert your holdings from a loan into shares of stock is a very valuable one and may be worth a great deal of money. There are so many convertible securities with various conversion privileges that it is impossible to generalize about the details of any of them. Some have short conversion periods, others have conversion periods beginning many years ahead. Most have the right of redemption. Generally, the price of a convertible fixed-interest security will rise or fall along with the movement of the stock, and will generally yield less than the same company's senior fixed-interest security.

As an investor, you should be very wary of buying convertible bonds at prices substantially above the level justified by the company's senior fixed-interest security—particularly where the conversion rights expire not many years ahead. You must understand thoroughly the mechanics of this investment before you trade the safety of a senior security for the subordinated convertible one. However, there is no question that a well-thought out plan of investing in convertibles may give you the yield you need, plus a bite at the equity apple.

Remember, knowing your way around the bond market is similar to knowing the stock market. This is a sophisticated market where you don't invest blindly. And again, you should be wary of brokers; they have their own interests to protect. On balance, however, the bond is where you should be looking today for the best yield and the best hedge against inflation. Like stocks, don't stay forever in one situation if the economics of the fixed-interest securities looks bad. Keep your eye on the company, and also on interest rates and general economic conditions.

FIXED-INTEREST INVESTMENTS

As everyone knows, it's very important to keep at least part of your capital in a suitable cash investment so that you always have cash available in case of emergency. Although stocks are reasonably liquid, we've already shown why it's unwise to rely on them as a source of emergency cash: If you are forced to sell when the market is down, then you lose money.

On the other hand, it doesn't make good financial sense to have too much ready cash, since cash can only grow if it is invested. The best solution is probably some fixed-income investments, but before deciding which ones, you should always consider the following elements:

1. *Yield.* The yield is the basic interest rate. It is either a "yield to maturity," which means the amount you will earn, expressed in a percentage, if you hold the security to the end of its term; or a "current yield"—what is yielding to you if you buy at the prices quoted; or "average yield," based on the assumption that you will hold until maturity but taking into account the fact that with many fixed-interest securities, such as bonds, there are sinking funds or other redemption provisions that will give you some of your money back sooner than the end of the term. For the private investor, yield is usually the most important factor in making a decision to invest in a fixed-income investment.

2. *Redemption.* Sometimes a private investor will purchase a fixed-interest security in order to be sure of receiving a known sum at a particular time, with a good income return in the meantime. For example, if you will need to provide a cash sum at a certain date because of bank borrowings or other obligations, a fixed-interest security, with a redemption date that coincides with the date on which you need the money, is ideal.

With a security that has a public market, of course, you can sell it on the market before the redemption date, but the amount you receive back, principal and interest, will be subject to the market risk of the purchase. For example, if you buy bonds when interest is high and don't hold them to maturity, these same bonds, when interest is lower, will generally bring you less on the market than you paid, and vice versa. The market risk is the economic interest rates, which are outside of your control.

Held to maturity, however, a fixed-interest security will pay the yield and give you back your principal, assuming the entity does not go bankrupt. A small risk, admittedly, but you must remember the thousands of small investors who put their savings into New York City.

3. *Accrued Interest.* The accrued interest is the interest owed to the seller at the time he sells his security. This must be paid by the buyer at the time of purchase, but he gets it back, either on the interest due date, or when he sells the security, or when the security matures.

BANK DEPOSITS

The simplest form of investment is in an interest-bearing account with a bank. In the United States, interest may now be paid on checking accounts. But higher interest rates are still paid on regular savings accounts. You can have a savings account at a savings bank or at a commercial bank. Or you could buy a certificate of deposit at a commercial bank if you have the minimum amount, which varies from bank to bank.

The forms and variety of accounts are too numerous to go into here, but generally the worst deal is a savings account at a commercial bank. For political reasons, a savings account at a savings bank now pays more than a savings account at a commercial bank, the yield differential ranging from 1/4 percent to 1/2 percent. The time factor is the important element; generally, the longer you leave your money, the higher the interest.

Although commercial banks are the worst places for straight savings accounts, that's where millions of people leave their savings. They do, however, pay the best rates on certificates of deposit, which are merely fancy savings accounts for the rich, if you can meet the minimum requirement.

Rates always change, but you can be sure you'll get the lowest rate possible with the banks because borrowing your money at a low rate of interest and lending it out to me at a higher rate is how they make their profits. There is not much advice we can give, except that you should ask for the longest term, if you don't need the money. At least that way you get a fixed rate and, again, if yields are high when you put your money in, you can enjoy the high yield even if rates come down. If yields are low and you think they are going higher, then stay in short-term deposits and invest long-term when rates move up.

It's a fun game, but one you will never actually win. However, nobody, in years, has lost his money in a bank in the United States; at least you will get your interest and principal when you are supposed to. Some banks pay a little more than others, but since only the *maximum* rate is regulated, not the minimum, be careful of the local bank if you are in a small town or a suburban area. The big city banks are always competitive and therefore the best place to get the highest yield or rate.

Savings-bank deposits are an attractive invest- ment for the average nonthinking investor, but probably aren't of much interest to you. If you do have such an account for children or grandchil- dren, though, make sure you understand the no- tice requirements which may apply before you can withdraw your money; with many such ac- counts, there is a penalty for early withdrawal.

Since savings banks can only lend on house mortgages, the best thing that can be said for them is that, if you leave your money in a given savings bank, it's just possible that you will get a better hearing if you want a mortgage or if you intend to buy a vacation house. The local savings bank may be the place to begin a small relation- ship.

A GOOD IDEA THAT BANKS WILL BE AGAINST

An investment in fixed-interest securities that moves with the prime rate or with treasury-bill auction rates is every investor's dream because it would give you the best of both worlds. Of course, you can make a killing by guessing which way the interest rates will go, but there are many times when you need to have your money in one of these kinds of investments for the sake of liquidity, rather than switch around.

Admittedly, certificates of deposit ("time de- posit,") do give you liquidity, but each time they come due you have to gamble on whether to invest short-term in case rates go up, or long-term in case they go down—and each time you run the risk of backing the wrong one.

Now, the Federal Deposit Insurance Corporation has proposed to allow certain banks to offer "time deposits" with interest rates pegged to treasury-bill auction rates. The proposal would apply to FDIC-insured commercial and mutual savings banks that aren't members of the Federal Reserve system, and would cover deposits of at least $1000 left with the bank for a minimum of two years. The FDIC has claimed that the "variable-rate time deposits" it is proposing "offer distinct advantages both to banks and to their customers." At the same time, though, it admits that it is only making the proposal now because interest rates in general are low and, therefore, the banks are less likely to offer any significant opposition.

A spokesman for the Federal Reserve has said that the Fed "doesn't feel ready at this time" to adopt a similar plan, though it's understood that it wants to consider all the alternatives before issuing a proposal. Under the FDIC proposal, the rate on variable-rate time deposits at commercial banks would vary quarterly, depending on the rates on thirteen-week treasury bills in the preceding quarter. Specifically, the rate would be arrived at by averaging out the coupon rate at the Treasury's weekly auction of thirteen-week bills during the four weeks leading up to the first day of the third month of each quarter. The rate would be published in the first five days of the third month of each quarter, giving the banks about twenty-five days to advertise the new rate before it took effect. The rate for mutual savings banks would be ¼ percentage point higher than the rate for commercial banks.

To protect depositors, banks would be allowed to set a minimum rate below which rates couldn't fall, but the floor couldn't be lower than 4½ percent. Banks also could set a ceiling rate as long as they disclosed the ceiling in their advertising and in deposit contracts.

The FDIC says the variable-rate deposits would be less expensive for banks than for four-year and six-year fixed rate deposits they currently offer, though at times the rates on variable-rate deposits would be higher than those on passbook savings accounts.

They also point out that, because the deposit could be at little as $1000 and would be insured, depositors could find the variable-rate deposits "an attractive alternative to investments in Treasury bills and other short-term securities."

COMMERCIAL PAPER

Commercial paper is another area best left to the professionals. The yield on commercial paper is higher than bank deposits—generally by between ½ and 1½ percent—and as you should know by now, higher yield means higher risk. In this case you are in effect lending money to a company engaged in the finance business, and that's risky. But just how risky?

You should try to find out the *exact* nature of the business the company is engaged in before you do anything else, and generally steer clear of any company offering interest rates that are substantially higher than those available elsewhere.

In order to pay you a higher rate of interest, they must be charging their customers a higher-than-average rate, and the only borrowers prepared to pay the premium are those who can't get money at the usual rates—in other words, above-average risks!

It is an area fraught with danger. Even companies offering the same rate can prove vastly different in terms of risk, so unless you have real knowledge of the field yourself, you must allow yourself to be guided by the experts, the banks and specialist brokers, which means you will be manipulated.

If you must invest in commercial paper, then it's best done short-term as a stopgap between other investments.

MONEY-MARKET SECURITIES

Money-market securities are the short-term obligations of various borrowers, including the United States Treasury, other federal agencies, state and local governments and many others. Almost all of these securities are substitutes for bank deposits. The difference between the securities is the element of risk; the lower the yield, says the market, the less the risk. United States treasury bills are considered the virtual equivalent of cash. Short-term federal-agency issues are next to treasury bills in marketability and safety. Short-term-tax-exempt obligations are also quite liquid, but here the risk is greater (or so we learned after the New York City fiasco), depending upon the issuing agency.

Also considered money-market investments are the large commercial banks' certificates of deposit (over $100,000); commercial paper, which we have dealt with above; bankers acceptances in denominations of $25,000 and up; and federal funds and Eurodollars, of which more later. Almost all of these investments are for the rich because of the high minimum requirements. They generally are higher yielding than investments of similar types without the large minimums in savings banks and other institutions.

Today, if you want to play this game, you can, but to meet the minimum requirements you have to participate in a pooled fund. Of course, you pay a fee for the service, but, on balance, these various kinds of pooled funds, the no-load variety, are very good investments if you want the professional's yield and do not have the minimum requirements yourself. These funds are highly regulated but the risk is minimal. Your banker or broker is the source of these kinds of securities.

The most difficult part of dealing in money-market securities as an investment is the fact that the yields run with the economy and the market, and unless you are talking about a long-term investment for, say, a year, and you have a lot of capital to invest, most banks or brokers won't bother with you. Most of these kinds of securities are for the institutional investor or very wealthy individuals. However, they are worth the trouble it takes to understand the market and find a good broker or banker because of the higher yields. In dealing with cash or equivalents like money-market securities, the yield is of paramount importance and ½ percent here and 1 percent there will, at the end of the period, make a great deal of difference to your spending fund.

THE TAX-EXEMPT MUNICIPALS

The great difference between these investments and all others is their tax-free nature. They are designed for the lazy rich who don't want to worry about tax shelters or investment strategies. If you are only in the 30-percent tax-bracket, a 7-percent tax-free yield is equal to a taxable yield of 10 percent, but in the 70-percent bracket it is the equivalent of a taxable yield of 23.34 percent— quite a hefty inducement!

Until 1975, these investments were also considered risk-free, the theory being that a United States state, city, town, village or any of the various authorities simply could not go broke. We have learned differently with the New York City crisis. Those of our friends who lived through it had the fright of their lives. Like us, they listened to the so-called professionals and always bought tax-frees whenever their earned income was up and they ran out of tax shelters. This used to be one of the best games in town, but not anymore. The risk factor has changed completely in the last twelve months, and, certainly, you need to be extremely careful with anything coming out of New York State.

The plight of New York City is the worst, but it's by no means unique. The balance of power is tipping away from obligations issued by the cities, towns and villages. Citizens are growing wary— and weary—of bad management by their local governments, and without federal assistance to shore them up, there is a serious question of survival.

Thus, what used to be a safe investment in a government body, whether state or local, is no longer safe and you must consider very carefully the benefit of the tax-free nature of the obligations against the very real risk of losing not only your interest but your principal, too. Indeed, the whole future of tax-free obligations is not too promising for the individual investor and has to be watched carefully.

If you give credence to what local government leaders say, you might conclude that we are wrong. On the other hand, to be forewarned is to be forearmed. It has been clear for some time that the management of many local governments is very poor, and a badly managed local government, like a badly managed company, must ultimately be heading for disaster. It's been obvious for some years that New York City was rocketing toward economic collapse, but nobody did anything about it until it was too late.

It's a matter of opinion, of course, but we no longer have any faith in tax-frees and would rather take our chances on the taxable side of the street.

INDIRECT INVESTMENTS

Indirect investments are another lazy man's way of trying to make money. Instead of investing in stocks yourself, you invest in a mutual fund, which in turn invests in stocks on your behalf. Instead of investing in bonds, you put your money into a bond fund; instead of cash investments, a dollar fund; and so on. For a fee, you have professionals making your investment decisions and purchases for you.

Don't confuse this, though, with making use of an investment *adviser* who acts merely as your counselor, not as a principal, in any transaction.

(At all costs avoid a "discretionary" account, in which you give your adviser or agent full or partial authority to buy and sell your stocks or bonds without your specific consent. Always insist on being sent a list of his recommendations, and consider each one before you tell him to go ahead and buy or sell.)

If you haven't the time to spend on making your own investments, then a top-notch investment counselor is worth his weight in gold and is an infinitely better proposition than any mutual, bond or dollar fund. For an annual fee, based on a small percentage of your investments' total value, an investment counselor will make all your investment decisions for you, subject to approval, and tailor them to your individual needs, something no fund can ever do. And don't be misled into thinking that investment counselors aren't interested in small investors. Some established firms are cutting the minimum account they'll manage to $10,000, and a growing number of banks are also taking on small accounts.

Many people who did invest in mutual or bond funds did so because they felt there was somehow safety in numbers, but, of course, in the stock-market slump between 1972 and 1975, the stock their funds invested in went down just like everyone else's. Many investors feel bitter about their funds' performance, but they have only themselves to blame. If you allow someone else to decide what to do with your money, then you must accept the consequences. Most people would probably have done just as well—or badly—by selecting their own investments and, what's more, they'd have saved themselves a fee which, in the end, only bought them someone to blame for their investments' poor performance.

If you are investing in a fund, make sure that the fund you're investing in is a "no-load" fund. In a "load" fund sold to you by your broker or a salesman, you pay a sales charge, or a "load." This is a one-time commission, in addition to other costs, which is paid up front and adds substantially to your costs. In a no-load fund, you eliminate the salesman, and thus the commission, and buy on your own. These funds, if otherwise well managed, are the best buys. The long-term records of the no-load funds compare favorably with those of the load funds, so don't be taken in; the lack of a sales charge has nothing to do with the caliber of the fund's management. In money funds, which we do recommend if you have a small amount of cash to invest, you can also find a no-load fund that's as good as any load fund.

Most people recommend funds because of professional management, federal regulation, convenience and liquidity. We do not—because, while they may be convenient and liquid, the management is often anything but professional. If a small sum of money is involved, the difference in results may not be great, but if you're thinking of investing a lot of money, you can get better advice from a professional counselor and your own judgment.

Nobody would disagree that over the short term, 1969 to 1974, most of the mutual funds had dreadful records, and most of their personnel were downright unreliable. In the long run, who knows? In our opinion, you would have been better off in a savings bank. The hedge funds of the 1960s were a disaster, as many investors found out; they lost as much as 40 to 50 percent of their value. The hot shots who ran them may have gotten all the publicity, but we'd never let them within a mile of our money.

The "closed-end" funds have been a disaster because you lose your liquidity, and while they operate like "open-end" mutual funds except that there are no redemption rights, their performance has been anything but good. Most of them are in the hands of management who don't have to prove themselves professionally by performance, and that in itself is a reason to stay away.

The real danger of indirect investments is that you are lured into thinking that you have a slice of the moneymaking market action as well as security, only to discover, perhaps, that you'd have done better to leave your money in the local savings banks. The bond funds and money-market funds, which are relatively new, invest in various types of banks or money instruments. In recent years, the yields of such funds have often been better than leaving your money in a savings bank, but they have yet to be tested in a really low-interest market. Again, the management is all-important, for you are buying their professional advice for a fee. We think, on balance, that with a little work you can do as well as they can, and avoid potential problems.

INSURANCE

The choice of programs offered by insurance companies today is wide, but if you are looking at insurance as a means of making your money grow, you're looking in the wrong place. On balance, any insurance program is merely an indirect investment with all the problems that entails, compounded by not very good, second-tier management. Insurance should be purchased for protection, and nothing else. A straight term policy, where you buy protection at the lowest rate, is far and away your best bet. Forget about the investment features. You must have protection for your family in case you die and leave them to handle all the problems that you created and only you could solve. Insurance to cover debt, insurance to cover marital settlements, insurance to protect your children and give them a start—they are all worthwhile ways to spend your money. But the best way is still to buy straight protection, at the lowest competitive rate, and do your own investing.

Another new idea—actually an old idea revisited—is the annuity policy. According to the *Wall Street Journal* (May 2, 1977), the smart money is going into insurance *vis-à-vis* an annuity. Specifically, insurance that yields a return as high as 7 or 8 percent with income taxes deferred for as long as you tie up your money. This insurance is known technically as a single-premium deferred-annuity contract. The plan is recommended for investors who consider it prudent to hedge more volatile investments with savings or other minimum-risk, fixed-income assets. The annuity can also be used as an estate-planning device, and also offers good tax deferment. While all the details are not yet clear, it looks like a great idea for the insurance industry and something that is worth looking into with your insurance broker.

THE EURO-CURRENCY MARKET

The development of the Euro-currency markets has been one of the most important innovations in international financial activity during the past decade. In simple terms, what it means is that commercial banks accept interest-bearing deposits in, and international companies sell bonds denominated in, a currency other than that of the country in which they operate. The Euro-currency markets have no national boundaries and therefore operate outside many of the existing exchange-control regulations and the rigidities in national banking practices. This has allowed participants, both the seller and the buyer, to take advantage of the international and national interest-rate differentials caused by the world economies.

Because of the dominant position of the U.S. dollar in international finance, the Eurodollar market has been the dominant market. It was the first to develop and is now larger than all other Euro-currency markets combined. In many ways the market is not unlike the bond market in the United States or the bank deposit system operated by U.S. banks, but, up to now, information about the specific companies selling Eurobonds has been hard to come by. The literature on the Eurodollar market is sparse because up to now it has served mainly the big institutional investors and the banks themselves. There has always been an aura of mystery about the market and not many U.S. banks or brokers will recommend it—once again, self-interest is playing a significant part—but in fact, for the individual investor, it has the greatest potential.

Americans can buy existing issues of Eurodollar bonds and invest in Eurodollar deposits through the major banks operating outside the country. Now, even Moody's Investor Service and Standard & Poors, both financial rating houses, have begun to rate Eurodollar bonds. Securities salesmen and the American banks have been re-

ceiving large numbers of small American orders.
Merrill Lynch, the giant stockbroker, has recently
outlined the virtues of Eurodollar bonds to its
sales force after underwriting and making markets in the issues abroad for years.

The difference between a Eurodollar deposit
and a Eurodollar bond is the same as that between
a deposit invested with a U.S. bank and a bond
bought on the U.S. bond market. Merrill Lynch
points out that, in selling Eurodollar bonds in the
United States, caution is required because many
of the borrowers—foreign companies—are unknown to most Americans.

Here is an opportunity to expand your knowledge and maybe find an investment that most
investors in the United States have not yet heard
about. Investors in Europe, the Middle East and
Africa, by contrast, know most of the borrowers
and have long preferred steady income to potential capital gains in the stock market. Interest
rates in the Eurodollar and Eurobond markets
are generally higher—they have to be, to attract
dollars from the United States where they are
safer than they would be anywhere else in the
world.

Unquestionably, the risk in the Euro-currency
market is higher (Euro-currency deposits are not
protected by deposit insurance the way U.S. domestic bank accounts are), but, in this case, it's
a risk well worth taking.

Risk isn't the only reason that yields are higher
in Euro-currency markets; convenience has a good
deal to do with it, too. There is no real reason why
deposits in the Chemical Bank, New York, and
the Chemical Bank, Zurich, shouldn't carry the
same degree of risk, but you'll get considerably
more on your money in Zurich than in New York.

Why? Because for most Americans banking in Zurich is much less convenient, so potential investors need to be wooed with higher yields.

The difference between Eurodollars and Eurobonds, from your point of view, is much the same as the difference between any money deposit and any bond, and the deciding factor may well be the degree of liquidity you need. With a Eurodollar deposit, you get your money at the end of the term, be it overnight, thirty days, ninety days or five years from the date of your investment. With a bond, if you have to sell before maturity to raise cash, you run the risk of receiving a lower price than you paid, if interest rates have dropped in the meantime.

The demand for cash, it used to be said, arises out of the needs for convenience and security, and thus produces a lower yield. With the short-term Eurodollar bonds, of course, convenience isn't a factor, but security is. Many companies in Europe, however, are as strong or stronger financially than the banks. (The same is true in the United States.)

Since U.S. dollar deposits are automatically included in the U.S. banking system (regardless of who owns them), the holders of U.S. dollars always have the option of leaving their deposits with U.S. banks as an alternative to placing them in the Eurodollar market. The fact that there are no currency-exchange controls for U.S. citizens, however, means that you can invest $1 million in Eurodollars tomorrow, if you choose to, which in turn means that the Eurodollar market has an extremely flexible supply of funds and that there is complete freedom of movement. Furthermore, the minimum rate paid on Eurodollar deposits must always be higher than the minimum rate paid on equivalent deposits in the United States; otherwise there would be no advantage in placing deposits in the Eurodollar market.

As in the United States, banks set different standards, but if you shop around you'll find many banks that will take as little as $5000 in Eurodollar deposits, especially the foreign banks operating in the United States who are hungry for deposits. Generally, U.S. companies with comparative bond issues selling on the New York Stock Exchange and in the Eurobond market pay a higher yield in the Eurodollar market than they pay on the domestic market. If they want to tap this market, they must meet the higher-yield demand.

There is an additional important hedge available in the Euro-currency market. Since it involves a series of markets dealing in foreign currency, you can buy bonds designated in Swiss francs, deutschemarks, French francs or what have you. Thus if you believe in the Germans, as I do, you can buy a Eurodollar bond in deutschemarks, which will give you a better yield and a chance to own deutschemarks. The same goes with Swiss francs.

Unlike straight currency investments, which we don't recommend (more of that later), we do believe in Euro-currency bonds in certain designated currencies, like Swiss francs and deutschemarks. In this way you can, if you wish, speculate in currency but with much greater safety. In general, however, if you have dollars, we recommend that you stay in dollars in the Eurodollar or Eurobond market. For example, if you want to speculate on the theory that England will survive, you will find bonds of English companies in dollars selling in the Eurobond market at much higher rates than those of their American counterparts.

Of course in the international market the demand for things English is limited, so if you need liquidity, be careful; if you don't hold the bond until maturity, you'll find the market very thin and the bond hard to sell. In fact, be cautious with all Eurodollar bonds because the markets are not as liquid as the American domestic markets for the same company's bond. In general, however, this is an area where we believe you can find good fixed-interest investments at higher yields; certainly in the Eurodollar market the higher rates are worth any time and trouble spent in finding out how they work. Note also that, unlike U.S. securities which are usually registered in the owner's name, Eurobonds are issued in bearer form, without any record of the holder. Thus Eurobonds can be salted away in a Swiss bank and earn interest beyond the reach of potential creditors. It is estimated that a third of newly issued Eurobonds are sold to clients of Swiss banks.

CURRENCY SPECULATION

For "investment in foreign currency" read, "currency speculation." But whatever you call it, it's another game only for the stouthearted. Over the past few years, headlines about currency crises and the villains of the peace—the speculators—have become, first, a monthly, then a weekly, and now almost a daily occurrence.

Generally the scenario is as follows: The Apaches (investors/speculators) surround the fort (the Central Bank) while the gallant defenders come near to exhausting their ammunition (gold and currency reserves) in holding off the attack. As often as not, the Apaches inexplicably ride off just as things are getting really tense, but occasionally they do breach the walls and reduce the fort to ashes, leaving the survivors to regroup on new ground in the rather dubious safety of a ring of covered wagons!

In the old days—good or bad, depending on your point of view—when exchange rates were fixed, there was practically no speculation in currency except by a few old established professionals. Rates were defended with the sort of determination that John Wayne applied to keeping the Stars and Stripes fluttering. Now, however, all that has changed. With the world's major currencies "floating"—and in some cases, like the dollar, sinking fast—you can gamble on the German mark, the French franc, even the pound if you always go for rank outsiders.

Inflation has made all the difference, and these days the devaluation or revaluation of a currency reflects on the country's economic performance. Today some currencies are so finely balanced that a strike by a handful of men in a key industry can wipe literally millions off their value.

You can speculate which way a country's economy will go, and the currency will go with it. But it's rather like being in Las Vegas, except that if you have a telephone at hand you don't have to stir from your livingroom couch. The worldwide currency game is like a giant crap game, except that in addition to the gambling instinct of a Big Jim Brady you need a Ph.D. in economics and politics to understand the heads of state, their psychology and egos, as well as the fundamental economic setup of the countries involved and the cross-currents of international politics.

In short, the areas of uncertainty are great and unless you want to become a trader and cover your position every night, you'll need nerves of steel. To invest in currency, without hedging on the other side, is almost suicidal. We tried it in silver some time ago, and our advice is, "Stay away, unless you have a broker you trust implicitly and who has a proven track record." Even then, think hard: If he's that good, why is he still a broker? If his track record was really that impressive, then he'd be a very rich man with no need to take you or anyone else on as a client.

SWISS BANKS—TO BE USED BY THE SOPHISTICATED

Most of us have heard about Swiss banks—paperback novels are full of them—but very few of us understand them. A Swiss bank is of little use to you unless you do a lot of business in Europe or are interested in better advice, and maybe a better yield. By Swiss banks, we don't mean just those originating in Switzerland but those operating there. For example, practically every major American bank has an office in Switzerland, be it Zurich or Geneva, which is, in all respects, operated as a Swiss bank. If you are interested, then using an American bank in Switzerland is by far the best method. At most of these banks you find people who know the European way but, since they have been trained in America, also understand the American way.

The Swiss banker can be useful to you if you

want to invest in a foreign country, if you are interested in Euro-currency deposits, Euro-currency bonds, currency transactions or the stocks sold on foreign stock exchanges. A good Swiss banker is a combination of a good American stockbroker and your local banker. Having a Swiss banker is most convenient for those who live abroad, but generally not worth the trouble if you spend most of your time in America, as Euro-currency deposits and Euro-currency bonds can be handled by your local bank, without ever having to go to Switzerland.

As for bank secrecy, perhaps as a way of avoiding U.S. taxes, forget it; it isn't worth the time and effort and on balance can only do you more harm than good. Swiss bankers are not interested and neither should you be. Avoiding taxes through a Swiss bank account does not work—never has—and is one of the great misconceptions held by Americans who have never dealt with a Swiss banker or, for that matter, lived abroad. If a Swiss banker even suspects tax evasion, he may voluntarily waive banking secrecy and permit the government tax authorities to examine the client's bank accounts. In fact the Swiss government has put before the lower house of Parliament a bill that would make "serious" tax evasion by both citizens and noncitizens in Switzerland a criminal offense. Its ultimate passage is far from certain since the lower house has already rejected two similar proposals in 1960 and 1969, but its chances seem a little better this time as the upper house has already approved the new bill's proposals. The Swiss finance minister, in introducing the bill, said, "Theft is theft and tax fraud is the same kind of thing."

Tax evasion is already a civil offense in Switzerland, punishable by a fine, but the new bill is concerned with what the government calls "major and serious tax fraud." In the past its opponents have argued successfully that making tax evasion a crime would affect Switzerland's banking-secrecy regulations; the government could demand information from a bank to obtain proof of tax evasion, whereas in the past the government has always been required to present evidence of a crime *before* they could obtain information from the banks.

In the last few years, any American would-be tax evader has been squeezed from both sides. The Internal Revenue Service has been cracking down on suspected tax evasion through foreign bank accounts, and from all indications they have made a lot of headway. Since 1970 the federal income-tax form has contained the question, "Did you at any time during the taxable year have any interest in . . . a bank, securities, or other financial assets in foreign countries . . . ?" If the answer is yes, then the taxpayer must fill out a form giving the details of his foreign holdings. If a taxpayer falsely answers no, he has committed a crime.

Let us emphasize that there is nothing that prohibits your holding these things, but you must disclose that you have them. If you use foreign accounts for legitimate purposes, you have no need to worry. If you don't, then you have big problems.

The Internal Revenue Service believes that merely putting this question on the tax return has discouraged many a potential tax evader from opening a Swiss account and may have frightened others into closing theirs. If that is the case, then it is for your own good, because unless you are going to use a Swiss account legitimately for investing, it's one of the greatest wastes of money there is. The Swiss know how to charge for the privilege of doing business in Switzerland.

Many bankers we have met have told potential investors in Eurodollar accounts that if they answer "yes" to the question about having a foreign account which is used for legal purposes they may be inviting an audit by the Internal Revenue Service. This is nonsense—lazy self-interest.

If you are an American and you want a foreign account, you can have one. You can open it through your local bank, preferably a major bank, or, if you wish, you can walk into a Swiss or foreign bank operating in your city and they will make the arrangements. In our experience, it is pointless to open a numbered account. If you are going to have a working account, it should be a simple, direct account that gives you bank statements and other evidence of activities for your tax records. A numbered account will only arouse suspicion, and besides it is very inconvenient. There is also the danger of someone else discovering the number of your account and systematically looting it. In fact, Swiss banks in America will not usually open a numbered account.

Swiss banks generally pay low interest on deposits, but that's because you are invested in Swiss francs which in themselves are considered an inflation hedge and therefore compensate for the yield. You should only consider a Swiss bank account as an investment vehicle—not for normal banking—to be used *only* if you want to diversify your investments and get into foreign securities or other kinds of foreign transactions.

In sum, the Swiss account is a vehicle to be used only with knowledge by the most sophisticated kinds of investors. On balance, it is the advice offered by the Swiss bankers in opening up alternative sources of investment that makes it worthwhile. And, even so, you can get practically the same advice today from a branch of an American bank operating in Switzerland—and as a bonus, their English is usually better.

6

THE ART OF LIVING RICH WITH ART

When people who know very little about us visit us at home, they usually stare at our paintings and sculpture, not knowing quite what to make of them—or us! What they don't understand at first is that they are in the presence of two art addicts, and, like any other addiction, once you're hooked, your whole life changes.

Art is now one of the most important activities in our lives, in three ways. First, we collect paintings, sculpture and graphics, which means that we buy things because we happen to like them and want to have them around us, regardless of whether they are cheap or expensive.

The second area of activity is similar, except that we combine collecting with investment and try to buy art we like but which we also believe will increase in value, just like other commodities, whether they are stocks, gold or real estate.

The third area of activity, and the most pleasurable, is working with young, as yet unrecognized artists and helping them to help themselves. We believe there are few more deserving people who can really benefit from a little help than young artists.

THE ART MARKET

Works of art are sold on what is strictly a free market in the sense that prices of the objects being bought and sold are regulated largely by demand and the extent to which they can be supplied. There is no tax on buying and selling in most countries (Paris is the exception, and the tax on auction sales is largely responsible for destroying the city's predominance in the art market and leaving the field open for London, New York, Vienna and Germany) and no artificial aids to price maintenance except the reserve prices placed on certain works at auction.

The market flourishes because it is free. Indeed the art market has enjoyed more prosperity since the war than almost any other, and it is significant that, whenever the economy is good, prices rise for works of art offered at auction. ·

Although objects like paintings, sculpture and graphics in which the art market deals have no real "utilitarian" value, they have always been regarded as an indispensable part of civilized life in every kind of society, from the most sophisticated to the seemingly primitive. For this reason, the art market is particularly sensitive to any kind of regulation and could only survive on anything like its present scale as a free market.

·DEFINING THE INVESTMENT IN ART

These days, the "art market" covers a wide variety of objects—antiques, tapestries, silver and so on —but since it's the area we know most intimately we shall concentrate on paintings, sculpture and graphics.

Works of art vary widely in quality, and these variations are often, but not invariably, reflected in the price paid. At this point the art market begins to exhibit marked differences from other markets. If you're buying an automobile, the price difference between a Mustang, say, and a Cadillac reflects a very real difference in performance, comfort, durability and, of course, status, all of which can be measured in objective terms. But in choosing between two paintings, the standards that are brought into play are almost purely subjective, based on the knowledge, experience and personal taste of the appraiser.

HOW TO BUY

Works of contemporary art are bought either directly from the artist or, more often, from the agent representing him, or at auction. The agent usually maintains a gallery for the exhibition of paintings, and charges a commission on sales as his remuneration. This commission is likely to vary with the status and popularity of the artist. Occasionally, if a young artist is unusually promising, less conventional agreements may be entered into; the gallery may pay a fixed annual retainer, for instance, in exchange for the sole right to sell the artist's work, and get their money back from profit rather than commission. Some galleries accept work for sale without an agreement extending beyond a single exhibition, and for this they charge a commission on sales plus an agreed proportion of expenses incurred for catalogs, publicity material, entertaining and general promotion.

Most artists begin by selling to friends and acquaintances, and by showing at exhibitions open to those whose work reaches a required standard. In the early stages of his career, before he is able to establish a general price level for his work, setting prices is a difficult problem because the strength of the demand is untested. Negotiation thus often plays a large part in arriving at a price, which will depend largely on the artist's own skill in promoting himself and impressing his personality on prospective buyers, as well as on the acumen of his agent in regulating the marketing of his work. The agent sometimes artificially curtails supply, only allowing work to be sold to selected buyers. A contemporary artist may be said to have "arrived" when his work realizes prices in the auction room closely related to those asked by the gallery handling his work, and to those obtained for the work of his better-known contemporaries.

The popularity of most contemporary artists rests on the establishment of an easily recognized, distinctive style that the public associates with them. Paintings departing from this style, or even from the usual subject matter, do not reach normal price levels, and may fall very much below them.

Buyers come into the art market for a variety of reasons, among which a love of the objects they are buying is a fairly important one, and certainly the most traditional. As long as there has been art, there have been collectors. Specialization in a particular item, like silver or procelain or bronzes, is a comparatively recent phenomenon, however, since such articles used to be simply a part of a general interior-decoration scheme. In comparison to the great Florentine art patrons of the Renaissance, like the Medicis, for instance, today's collections tend to be smaller, and the focus of attention has changed. But even so, collections of exceptional interest still tend to become known, and the fact that a well-known collector owns works by a particular artist becomes almost a Good Art Collecting Seal of Approval.

A collector does not acquire that kind of reputation overnight, of course, but, once gained, it will probably outlive him. Even now, objects from famous nineteeenth-century collections that still bear the owners' label sell more easily and at higher prices than comparable specimens without such a label.

If you are starting out as a collector, it makes sense to try to choose a subject—or an artist—not currently in vogue, because you will be able to buy while prices are low. It's possible that in building your collection of nineteenth-century American art, West African tribal art or the young artists of California, you will influence other collectors in the same direction. With increased interest, demand will also increase and prices will rise—bad news if you are still building your collection, but good news if you are ready to sell. Obviously, choosing an unfashionable area in which to collect is a gamble and should be undertaken with great care, but it is still possible to pull it off.

If you have a specialist collection to sell, the best way is through a well-produced catalog, sold in limited editions to fellow collectors and dealers. It's expensive to produce, but it usually enhances sale prices to a considerable extent.

If you are not buying direct from the artist or

his agent, then you can buy either at auction or from a dealer. If you buy from a dealer, you are usually paying the price the work would fetch in the auction room *plus* his profit and overheads.

A fair markup, we maintain, is 30 percent, but since few dealers are likely to tell you what they paid for the picture they are about to sell you, you'll need to have a good idea of what the price probably was in order to assess whether you are being taken to the cleaners or not. The best guarantee you have of a good deal is the dealer's reputation for fairness.

You should also remember that some "private collectors" buy at auction with the express purpose of reselling at a profit, so don't assume that because the man who is selling you a painting doesn't have a gallery he isn't going to try and get as much for his wares as he possibly can!

AUCTIONS

Auction-room activities may seem alarming at first, but it's really a question of learning your way around.

Auction houses vary widely in the quality of the service they provide. At the top are the established firms like Sotheby's in New York and London, Christie's of London and New York, Ketterer in Munich, the Dorotheum in Vienna, and many others in Geneva and other places in Switzerland. Such firms maintain a staff of experts in various categories, and their catalogs achieve a high standard of objectivity and accuracy in their descriptions of the works offered for sale. They receive objects for sale from almost every part of the world, and most are still sold to dealers, although private buying is beginning to account for an increasingly greater percentage, especially in the graphics field.

The auction house is the agent of the seller of the property, not the buyer, and will advise the seller on such questions as the reserve price (the price below which an item may not be sold) and the best method of presenting the item for sale. The house charges a variable rate of commission based on selling price and cost of handling, and to this are added any special expenses incurred, such as illustrations in the sale catalog.

Although the best auction houses employ expert staff, they specifically exclude in their conditions of sale any responsibility for faults, defects or errors in catalog description; the statements in their catalogs are expressions of opinion, not necessarily to be accepted as fact. It is your responsibility as the intending purchaser to examine the property offered, prior to the sale, to assure yourself of its condition and the correctness of the catalog description. However, if your purchase subsequently turns out to be a deliberate forgery and was wrongly cataloged, the conditions of sale give you the right to return it, usually within thirty days of the sale (that is, before the seller has been paid by the auctioneer), when the sale will be rescinded.

THE DEALERS

Like auctioneers, dealers vary widely in knowledge, competence and integrity. A good list can be found in *Fine Arts Market Place* by Paul Cummings (R. R. Bowker Co., 1975). The best achieve a very high level and are internationally known as authorities on their particular subjects. At this level, most tend to specialize in a few categories, passing on anything outside them to their colleagues. Their prices are apt to be based on demand as they know it rather than on cost, but as they tend to buy in large auction rooms in competition with other specialists, they are unlikely to acquire very much at prices conspicuously below current market value.

KNOWLEDGE—YOUR BEST GUIDE

The most important asset to anyone in the art market is a knowledge of painting, sculpture and graphics, which is only acquired through many years' study and experience. It is invaluable in two ways: first, in knowing when an item has been overlooked by other experts and is worth more than the price placed on it by its owner; and, second, in knowing what the potential demand (not necessarily the immediate demand) for the item could be.

Lord Stamp, a British economist of the 1930s, once said, "An item is worth what it will fetch," and nowhere is that more true than in the art market. Ask half a dozen "experts" what a particular painting will fetch at auction and you'll get half a dozen widely differing answers, because each expert has a different attitude toward the painting's potential. The only test, ultimately, is to put it up for auction, though even then the price it fetches is only valid for that particular time and place; offered for sale in another auction room the following day, it might fetch an entirely different price, and the deciding factor could be whether or not one particular collector was absent or present. Diane once picked up a real bargain at an art auction on the eve of Thanksgiving because all the big collectors who might otherwise have been there and pushed prices up were already out of town for the holiday.

Nevertheless, many paintings—perhaps most—are pretty consistent in the prices they realize. Books like *International Auction Records* by G. E. Mayer (Editions Mayer) and the monthly *International Art Market*, which publishes prices in the major auction rooms after the sales, have done much to bring an element of certainty into assessing prices. Of course, that does not mean it is becoming possible to fix prices, but it does mean that if you know what a similar work by the artist you are interested in fetched in London six months ago, you have a good idea of what would be a reasonable price to pay.

Price levels are also affected by fashion, because it influences demand. And as with fashions in music, literature, even clothes, many of the reasons behind the fluctuations in an artist's popularity have little to do with intrinsic merit. For example, very large canvases used to be unsalable because very few people had homes large enough to hang them, but that is no longer true. Renoir's nudes are always in great demand, partly due to an appreciation of his art, partly the perennial popularity of the subject, and partly because his style harmonizes extremely well with eighteenth-century French furniture in expensive, decorative homes, taking the place over a commode of the Boucher or Fragonard which might have hung there in the eighteenth century.

Of course, quality does play an important part in determining the value of a work of art—the difference in the prices realized at auction between specimens of good and bad quality, in the same generic group, is often wide—but it is extremely difficult to define what "quality" in terms of a particular painting or piece of sculpture actually means.

To become a reliable judge of quality one must see as much as possible, and know as much as possible, not only from reading books on the subject, but also from studying the objects themselves, trying to see the worst as well as the best. Eventually, notions of quality sort themselves out as a kind of continuum, with the best at one end and the worst at the other, specimens being marked off somewhere between the two points. If this spectrum is compared with auction prices, the two will usually agree tolerably well.

Journalists in search of sensational copy have fostered some widespread misconceptions about the dangers of forgery. True, there are a very large number of forgeries and reproductions in existence, but few of them are good enough to deceive anyone who knows the artist's genuine work, and even the best have a relatively short life. Forgeries are only a real danger to the uninformed, overenthusiastic buyer who, on the lookout for a bargain, buys from rather dubious sources.

It is now easy to get an education in the vagaries of the art market, as an investment. Books we recommend are Gerald Reitlinger's *Economics of Taste* in two volumes, the first dealing with paintings (published in 1961) and the second with objets d'art (1964). They trace the course of the market over the last two centuries or so in a

scholarly yet entertaining manner. You should
also read Richard H. Rush's *Art as an Investment*
(McGraw Hill), and Richard Blodgett's new book,
How to Make Money in the Art Market (Peter H.
Wyden, 1975).

Since World War II, investments in works of
art have had a better record than almost any other
form of investment, and there have been no major
recessions in *real* worth. During a time of economic gloom like the early 1970s the prices realized at auction were lower than in the late 1960s,
but that reflects more on the thinking of the seller
than on art as an investment. Works of art should
not be sold in a "down" market because, unlike
stocks, it is almost certain that they will regain
their value when the market turns up again. What
that means, of course, is that art should only be
bought when your cash flow is well provisioned,
and should be regarded as long-term, fixed assets,
with all the lack of liquidity that that implies.

THE ASSETS THAT MAY SAVE YOU

There were few collectors as ardent as Josef
Rosensaft. Mr. Rosensaft, a survivor of the Ausch-
witz and Bergen-Belsen concentration camps, was
a man to be reckoned with. He had two main mis-
sions in life; one, never to let the world forget
what had happened to the millions of Jews who
died in the Nazi concentration camps; and two,
to make money to buy impressionist paintings.
Starting with a small collection, he built one of
the major private collections of impressionist
paintings after World War II.

Sadly, as a result of some bad breaks in currency transactions in late 1975 and the liquidation of a small bank in Switzerland, Rosensaft became indebted to a number of leading banks in New York. Not willing or able to pledge his other assets, Rosensaft decided to give the banks a lien on his paintings. Normally, banks will not take paintings as collateral but Rosensaft was considered to be so sound financially that the banks went along. Just when he was attempting to make a comeback in the currency market, he died suddenly in London, leaving the banks, as it turned out, with only the paintings as their sole source of repayment.

While the bankers were quite nervous over paintings as collateral, the art market rose to the occasion and the Rosensaft paintings sold at near-record auction prices at Sotheby, Parke, Bernet in New York. Though not all of the paintings sold, because the reserves were quite high, the collection grossed $6.6 million, just below the record of $6.9 million for a single sale—in no event a distress sale!

A painting by Paul Gauguin, *Still Life with Japanese Woodcut*, was sold for $1.4 million, almost $300,000 more than Rosensaft paid for the painting from Bill Acquavella just a few years earlier. Citibank, who held a lien on the Gauguin, also sold a Pissarro for $190,000 and a Monet for $130,000. The Wells Fargo Bank of San Francisco received a total of $1.4 million for paintings they held.

We remember talking for Rosensaft shortly before his death, and the one thing he stressed was that, no matter how bad his financial problems were, he would not sell his collection. A painting, maybe, but not the collection. He kept saying that his only mistake had been not buying more pictures!

For a lot of speculators, the very illiquidity of paintings is a great safety device. In case after case, when trouble has developed with a man's investments, his paintings have ended up as his most enduring asset because, while he was tempted to sell or hock almost anything to get himself out of trouble, the banks would generally refuse to take the paintings as collateral.

HOW TO MAKE MONEY
USING THE BREAKUP TECHNIQUE

One of the best ways to make money in the art market is to use the breakup technique. While it can be done with paintings, it is probably simpler with graphics than anything else.

During the last ten years, many of the major artists, from Picasso to Chagall, have all done important sets of graphics—Chagall's set of Bible etchings, for example, or Picasso's *Vollard* suite. A set of the Bible etchings sells for anywhere from $70,000 to $80,000. They are hand-colored by the artist and signed with a monogram, "M. Ch." The edition is 105 mixed etchings, published by Teriade in Paris in 1956, and the original price in 1956 was probably around $5000.

By now, twenty years later, there are few complete sets left because Chagall, with his bright colors and well-known name, is one of the best-selling graphic artists in the world, especially in the United States. Any true collector of graphics has a few of Chagall's.

Suppose you're lucky enough to find a complete set of 105 pieces, as we did, out in the Midwest, and the asking price is $80,000. If you possibly can, buy! Not many people who collect graphics have $80,000 to spend, which is why they are so cheap—and believe it, $800 a graphic *is* cheap, since they retail at around $1600 each and the wholesale price is $1300. Any number of dealers or auction houses can move these for you at the $1300-a-piece price, $5000 at a time. With a set of Bible etchings, you should be out completely in about three months, with a profit of $400 each, or a total of $42,000. That works out to 50 percent on your money. Not a bad art investment.

You could do the same with the Chagall *Daphnis and Chloe* suite, 60 colored etchings from an edition of 250; or Picasso's *La Suite Vollard*, from 1939, considered to be one of his best graphics ever. The list in the graphics field is almost limitless, but be careful to pick things that move quickly because time, here, is money, and if you have to wait too long to break up the set you may find yourself with a long-term investment rather than a short-term one. If that should happen, however, you may come out even better, because as the suites by major artists disappear, you may have the only complete set left, which will then sell at premium to some museum.

In any case, make sure you know how to sell what you have bought. You might go in with a graphics dealer as your partner, for instance, but insist that he put up his half, or he won't have the necessary incentive.

This breakup technique is not limited to graphics. Collectors, scholars and students of music are grieving over the dismemberment of an extremely rare and precious manuscript of Mozart's —the score, in his own hand, of his *Andretter* Serenade (KV 167a–185). The manuscript came up for auction in February 1975 at Marburg, West Germany. It was knocked down for DM250,000, the buyer had to pay the auctioneer a fee of about 12 percent, and the whole deal cost about $100,000.

A consortium of Americans, led by a California dealer, bought the work and put it on show at the Antiquarian Book Fair in New York in April 1975. A price several times that paid at the auction was being asked, but the market in musical manuscripts is small and observers were not surprised that the manuscript failed to sell.

At that point the owners apparently decided that their investment would have to be recouped by selling the eleven-movement manuscript piecemeal. One movement has been bought by a collector on the Continent. One leaf with eighty-seven bars came up for auction at the Charles Hamilton Galleries in New York. It fetched $9000 from a "private United States collector."

The whole manuscript had 116 pages, so selling piecemeal in this way means that the consortium stands to make a very substantial profit. One difficulty involved in the breakup, though, is that movements do not start on separate pages, therefore separating the movements entirely is impossible. It is true that complete microfilm copies of the entire serenade exist so that scholars can establish exactly what Mozart intended.

A distinguished dealer in musical manuscripts says: "This was an absolutely ghastly thing to do. Every scholar and serious person must regard it as indefensible. What has happened is financial exploitation of what ought to be inviolable. That more people will be able to own and see the fragments is no excuse. I would never consider being

party to buying or selling portions of this manuscript, even indirectly. But now the deed has been
done, I cannot blame any collector or librarian for
seizing the chance to acquire an example of
Mozart's music in his own hand."

7

HOW TO SPEND YOUR MONEY
SUCCESSFULLY

CAN YOU AFFORD A DIVORCE?

Married couples now are divorcing at nearly twice the rate they were in the 1950s; roughly one in every three American marriages now ends in divorce. But census figures show roughly 75 percent of divorced women and 80 percent of divorced men remarry. "We're in a terribly overmarried society," anthropologist Margaret Mead observed in a 1971 article, "because we can't think of any other way for anybody to live, except in matrimony as couples." Everybody gets married—and unmarried—and remarried—but the vast majority of people are married to somebody most of the time.

All of this divorce and remarriage costs money. First, there is the cost of the divorce—the cost in dollar terms, that is, not bitterness, anxiety, loss of sleep and general psychological upheaval. The emotional and psychological repercussions of a divorce begin to fade after the first few months, but the financial ones linger on.

In almost any state in the United States, the husband pays all of the costs of the divorce, including the wife's legal fees, no matter who initiates the divorce. I remember speaking before a Long Island bar association on the opportunities for lawyers to make money from investments—and learning, to my complete surprise, that most suburban lawyers who used to support themselves on auto accidents (negligence), real-estate transactions, wills and trusts, now make most of their money from divorce proceedings.

In the case of simple divorces—divorces not involving children or the division of valuable assets—many couples have started using do-it-yourself "divorce kits." Furthermore, now that the U.S. Supreme Court has decided that lawyers can finally advertise, we are seeing more and more competitive advertising in the newspapers offering bargain-rate divorces only a few columns away from used-car ads.

Such simple and inexpensive divorces, however, are not available for those who have property and other assets that must somehow be equitably divided, and alimony, custody and child-support questions that must be settled. These are matters for lawyers, arguments and litigation. Even in California, where the division of property in a divorce is controlled by community property laws, I think you would be surprised at how much heat can be generated over adding up the property and deciding who gets what. And in states where community property laws don't apply, the scope for argument is obviously that much greater since, by law, neither the husband nor the wife is entitled to any of the other's property as part of any divorce settlement.

Naturally, her lawyer wants as much as he can get for his client—and for himself in terms of fees—and the husband wants to obligate himself to pay as little as he can get away with. That may sound heartless, but the key word is "obligate."

There is nothing to stop a man from giving his ex-wife and children more *voluntarily*, but, legally, he can't give them less.

One of the most striking changes in matrimonial actions since the late 1950s involves the woman's role in divorce. It used to be the husband who wanted the divorce; today, it is more likely to be the wife. Today, the woman is emerging, or so it seems, as a full partner and even a substantial breadwinner. Indeed, in a 1969 census survey, almost 8 percent of the wives earned more than their husbands—half again as many as the number who out-earned their husbands in a similar 1959 sampling. From this has flowed a new independence among wives in matrimonial actions.

If you hear that one of the big-name divorce lawyers is acting for a wife, then you know that the husband has a real battle on his hands. The battle is joined not only on a legal level but on a psychological one, too. The children, who usually remain in the wife's custody, are usually used as the driving wedge, and threats of litigation are held over the man's head as the final persuader.

In the past, rich husbands who failed to settle and went to court were almost invariably taken to the cleaners. Many of the judges were Catholics, and they also reflected society's view of the family as a permanent, intrinsically cohesive unit. Since men were almost always the initiators of divorce actions, the wife was often seen as the victim of her husband, who then had to compensate her handsomely for the loss of her marriage.

All that has now changed. In the last five years, judges have become younger and divorce has become as prevalent among their own relatives, friends, maybe their own sons and daughters—

and even themselves—as it is in other similar social groups. No matter how good a judge a man may be in the legal sense, there is nothing like personal experience for fostering an understanding of other people's plights. Even the Catholic church has taken a different attitude and more and more people in second marriages are continuing to live as Catholics.

A Man's View

The most important thing for a man to remember if he is involved in a divorce, or is contemplating one, is that he will almost certainly do better in a court of law today than he will by negotiating a settlement. Of course, if he can get a reasonable negotiated settlement, he should take it. The best settlement for a man is a one-time payoff for the wife (he can write it off as he would a bad deal or a bad investment) and good, rigid child-support payments for the children. He might just decide to pay all of his children's "reasonable" expenses and put an end to the arguments, but a fixed amount of money is better because then the children have to learn to live within a budget, which he can voluntarily increase as needed.

Monthly payments to an ex-wife as alimony, which is deductible to a man, or a ten-year settlement which is tax-free to her and not deductible to the man, are to be avoided. As time passes, the guilt fades, and a man will probably remarry, as most divorced people do. He will find each monthly payment harder and harder to make and will start to get behind—partly through necessity, because the costs of maintaining a second family will start increasing, but also because of the re-

sentment felt at having to pay one's whole life for
that one mistake. He will find himself in the courts
again and again, and it all costs money—in the
end he will have to pay not only the monthly payments but her lawyers' costs, as well.

So remember the old stock-market adage, "The
first loss is the best one." It applies as well to divorce as it does to the market. Aim at a one-time
payment, and be done with it.

The cost of a divorce, if the wife uses one of
the important matrimonial law firms, will be more
or less as follows: His fees should be under $3000.
Her fees, which of course the man pays, can run
between $5000 and $7500, depending—some
cynics might say—on how well or badly she does.

In most divorce cases, a fair amount of horse
trading goes on. The wife's lawyer will no doubt
start by saying that since husband and wife spend
$5000 a month together, the husband should con-
tinue to maintain his wife in the style to which she
has become accustomed. Ignore it. Even the courts
these days don't hold that view.

With the house and furniture the man leaves
her, perhaps worth around $100,000 after paying
off the mortgage (every matrimonial lawyer we've
ever met insists on this because they are such bad
businessmen!), the jewelry her husband bought
her over the years (another $50,000), the car
($6,000), clothes worth $25,000, and all the other
extras put in her name over the years, the woman
ought to be able to get along pretty well on $1000
a month, as long as the husband provides for the
children.

Each child shouldn't cost more than $150 a
month, plus camps at $1500 a year, school fees
at $2000 a year and vacations at another $500.

The $150 a month for each child should cover clothes, haircuts, allowances and medical expenses. Her monthly $1000 should cover the running of the house and food for the family.

Even with this minimum program, a husband will be paying out $12,000 for his ex-wife, plus $3600 for two children, plus at least $5000 for extras—a total cost of $20,500 a year. Obviously if a man can get away with a once-and-for-all lump sum payment of $100,000 instead of the monthly payments, he'll be getting a bargain. And beware of the "change of circumstance" ruling that allows a wife to request more money if she becomes needier or her ex-husband becomes wealthier.

Remember, alimony is tax-deductible—the government pays half—and the ten-year payout is not, which makes a difference to how much a man can afford to pay.

Remember also that the less a man is *obligated* to pay, the better his chance of coping with it all. He can always increase the amount he gives them, but it's very hard, though not totally impossible, to decrease it, once agreed.

A Woman's View

Having been amicably divorced myself and subsequently remarried to a man who lived through a bitter divorce, and having more divorced and remarried friends than friends who have remained married to one person, I personally think that a lump-sum settlement up front for the wife is the best course of action. Child support payments should be agreed upon with necessary inflation clauses to assure that payments keep up with the rising cost of living.

Although the lump-sum settlement might, at first, be anathema to the husband, it seems to be the quickest way to cauterize the wound of the divorce and stem the flow of venom that tends to recur with monthly regularity in situations where monthly payments have been part of the settlement. The monthly payment system puts a woman in a state of total bondage and dependency on the man. Furthermore, the woman can never be sure when the payments might be stopped for one reason or another, perhaps leaving her with little or no cash in hand for pressing expenses.

With a lump-sum cash settlement, a woman is given a stake in life commensurate with the wealth she shared with her husband and the number of years she spent living with him and helping him further himself. But receiving a cash settlement puts a huge responsibility on the woman to learn to manage and invest her funds to provide a steady income—a responsibility to which many women are not equal.

Many women have a bury-your-head-in-the-sand attitude toward money and business. They may not even know how much money their husband has, since they may have been confined to running the household while the husband took control of the really big expenditures. They may not know how a business is run, or think they are unable to understand complicated financial talk. But all a woman has to do is ask for explanations, either from her husband, a lawyer, a friend, a business associate, or anyone else suitable. It's not very difficult. During the divorce, however, she can be sure her husband and his lawyer will not want to divulge any secrets.

To protect herself for the future, a wife should

have started—long before the divorce—to ask her husband about his business and how it works. Ditto for the money and how it is handled. Otherwise, a woman will be in the dark about her own financial affairs when it matters most.

The best way to survive a divorce is to be prepared. If she's not, the first time she tries as a divorced woman, to use her old credit card, she may be in for a shock. She may not have any credit because the card is in her husband's name. And if alimony is her only income, she may find that stores are reluctant to accept that as a basis for issuing a new card in her own name. The key is for the woman to establish credit in her own name before the divorce happens.

The woman should also try to find a job as soon as possible, or go back to school, or even start her own business. The point is that she should pick up the pieces of her life and put them to work building a new life.

My view might seem a bit cynical to some, but it seems to me that there are two distinct groups of divorced women. The first make it their sole purpose in life to hate, to be vindictive, to victimize their children and generally make themselves bitter and miserable. The other group handle the divorce with maturity, tact, and good sense. They chalk it up as a bad experience, and seek psychological help when necessary, but the great difference is that they get on with the business of living, unlike the first group, who live in the past, rehashing old memories and stewing over past mistakes. Many of them use the divorce as a constructive experience enabling them to change their lives; they learn to enjoy their children more; they handle the husband's visitation rights with politeness and even consider it a chance for a little freedom; and they understand how important it is for the mental health of their children to maintain a good relationship with their ex-husband.

One more point: In the divorce settlement, a woman should try to get as many concrete items as possible, such as the house or car, for example. She may need to fall back on them if cash is short. Statistics show that while a woman will probably be awarded alimony, she will probably not collect it.

GIVING UP THE MANSION

How often do you hear the rich say, "Money doesn't really matter to me—after all, you can only wear one suit at a time, eat one dinner at a time, sleep under one roof . . ."? But there are suits and suits, dinners and dinners and, certainly roofs and roofs.

For most people, once they begin to make money, acquiring a new home to go with their new life-style and new aspirations usually takes top priority. These days, when you consider how much money is involved, house or apartment hunting should be undertaken with as much thought, care and effort as you'd give to any of your other investments. The days when you could still pick up the occasional "real bargain," or even a rent-controlled apartment, are over.

Until recently it made much better financial sense to buy, not rent, your home. It was one of the best hedges against inflation—your maintenance costs, after the initial payment, were usually lower, and over the years house prices had been continually rising. But in the economic upheaval of the early 1970s, that no longer holds true. Rising maintenance costs, and rising taxes, have made the cooperative apartment and the big suburban home an increasing drain on even the fattest pocketbooks.

In spite of the rising maintenance costs of cooperatives on the market today, owners of the real quality apartments can still ask very high prices for them, and since they tend to be very wealthy people themselves, they can afford to hold on to their property until they get them. The recent boom in the purchase of luxury cooperatives and condominums has been abetted by the worsening political situations in various foreign countries. Emigrés from the United Kingdom, France, Italy, Lebanon and various Arab as well as South American countries have been quick to purchase some of the more opulent and expensive properties.

Interestingly, the fact that these new American residents will be hit with U.S. income taxes seems to leave them undaunted. Either many of them have secreted their funds in a variety of foreign trusts or they have arranged to spend less than ninety days per year in the United States, thus avoiding the "resident" classification. Whatever the arrangement, there will surely be a collective shriek of agony uttered when the deadline for filing income-tax returns approaches, as it is apparent that many of them have failed to realize that paying U.S. income taxes is the price of the privileges they hoped to enjoy by moving to what they refer to as "the last bastion of capitalism and free enterprise."

In any case, the real estate agents can offer a range of apartments to suit every pocket—provided it's capacious—but if you want something really special, there's a splendid eighteen-room duplex at 740 Park Avenue for a mere $850,000, plus monthly maintenance charges of $3,385.75. If that seems exorbitant, please note that it has six master bedrooms, three maids' rooms, eight and a half bathrooms (the half is ideal for your eight-year-old son who only half-washes himself), a living room, dining room, two libraries, a servants' hall and a gymnasium, complete with sauna.

In addition to the usual extras included in the price—the chandeliers, ceiling and wall fixtures, mantels, air-conditioning and a stereo system that, alone, cost $18,000 to install—you also get 1740 shares of the capital stock in the building's corporation, which carries with it an approximately 25-percent tax reduction on your maintenance payments. So, if you are in a high enough tax bracket and are looking for something "a little bigger," it might be worth considering, if you are crazy!

If the big cooperative doesn't appeal and you're still looking for an alternative to the continually soaring costs of purchasing and maintaining a lavish home or apartment, how about letting someone else take care of all that for you?

There are also a number of residential hotels and luxurious condominium and cooperative apartment buildings that offer a variety of services. Olympic Towers, for example, on Fifth Avenue at 51st Street, offers catering services, banquet facilities, room service, a health club, wine cellar, a sophisticated communications lounge and a well-trained multilingual concierge, all designed to take the strain out of jet-set living.

The theory behind buildings like Olympic Towers was that the offices on the lower floors would reduce the building's maintenance costs for the cooperative apartment owners who lived upstairs in the tower. As an added convenience, many of the office renters could live in the building—a modern luxury version of living over the store. For New Yorkers who already live within easy commuting distance of their offices, the concept wouldn't have much appeal, but to the international businessman who comes to the city three or four times a year it is very attractive. Ideally, he can install the office downstairs and then, at the end of the day, take an elevator upstairs to a sumptuous apartment that conceivably could be charged to the company as a legitimate business expense!

About 77 percent of the purchasers are foreigners from South America, Europe and the Middle East. And the apartments *are* sumptuous. In Olympic Towers, for instance, designed by Skidmore, Owings and Merrill and built by Arlen Realty, the kitchens have marble floors, the bathrooms have marble floors *and* walls, as well as bidets, and the bronze glass, floor-to-ceiling windows take full advantage of the exquisite—and expensive—view.

As you'd expect, any prospective Olympic Towers tenant could be assured of a very nice class of neighbor—Mr. and Mrs. Jean-Pierre Marcie-Rivière, for instance, who also own homes in Paris, St. Moritz and St.-Jean-Cap-Ferrat, and Arthur G. Cohen, Arlen's chairman of the board.

The Madison Company—an affiliate of Madison Equities—believed so wholeheartedly in the condominium apartment idea that they built "Galleria" at 117 East 57th Street solely devoted to them. They placed advertisements in international publications in no less than eight languages, which gives you an idea of the kind of buyer they hoped to attract. But the sales did not materialize and their apartment occupancy was an appalling fraction of what they expected.

Condominiums *have* been enormously successful elsewhere, however, and it's not merely property companies and developers who are exploiting the concept. In March 1976 the Museum of Modern Art announced plans to build a luxury condominium tower atop their present building on West 53rd Street, which would double the existing museum space *and* provide much-needed income to offset the museum's deficits. The museum is working with the Arlen Realty and Development Corporation on the new venture, budgeted at around $40 million, and will have final approval on the building's design, currently being prepared by the St. Louis–based firm of Hellmuth, Obata and Kassabaum.

Certainly a condominium apartment over the Museum of Modern Art is an extremely attractive proposition for any art lover. One would not only be living in a building conforming to the highest standards of modern design, but also be able to say to guests, quite truthfully, "The Picassos are downstairs."

DON'T BUY FURNITURE—BUY ANTIQUES

When it comes to decorating your home, instead of ordinary furnishings, consider antiques. There is no limit to what you can choose from, and cities like New York have no shortage of experts only too happy to help you spend your money. No matter whether your taste is for European, Oriental or early American furniture, there are plenty of specialized dealers ready to cater to it.

All the experts, regardless of their specialty, agree that the wisest decision is always to buy the very best you can afford. It may seem like extravagance, but it isn't. Buying antiques is an investment, even though that isn't always the motive in buying them.

Here are just a few of the experts in the antique world. Ruth Constantino, owner of the Connoisseur, Inc., on Madison Avenue, is a purist who believes in signed pieces. "Always buy authenticity," she maintains. "If chosen with exceptional care and knowledge, antiques are better than securities, but they are not always quickly negotiable." In her shop, you will find signed pieces by *menuisiers* like Reuze and *ébénistes* like Cresson, with price tags starting at around $5000. Among her clients are Charles Allen, the Metropolitan Museum of Art, most of the Goulandris family, Stavros Niarchos and Mrs. John D. Rockefeller, Jr.

Joseph Lombardo, who lives above the store in a beautiful New York town house in the East 50's, specializes in eighteenth-century antiques, with a sprinkling of modern pieces to lighten the effect and make it more "livable." He and his partner Eddie Harmon are among the few antique dealers who appreciate the beauty of modern art and encourage their clients to collect what pleases them rather than insisting on their cramming their walls with matching period paintings.

Garrick Stephenson specializes in eclectic decorating and his tastes include English, French and Oriental furniture and accessories, for a very attractive polyglot look.

Martin Zimet of French & Company jets regularly to the international auctions to acquire some of the finest antiques in the world. Often he flies to foreign auctions to bid on behalf of clients who wish to acquire specific pieces while remaining anonymous. Mr. Zimet's credits include some of the major pieces in the late J. Paul Getty's collection of furnishings.

Frederick Victoria is a dealer who loves his work so much that he tends to fall in love with the pieces he buys and winds up keeping some of them, rather than selling them to his clients.

Joel J. Wolff is perhaps the prime source of superb English furniture. He was brought up in England, where his father dealt in antique furniture. His London shop having been destroyed in the war, Mr. Wolff came to New York in 1950, where his credentials have made him one of the most sought-after dealers among the rich who want to re-create the serenity and charm of an English manor house in New York City.

While initially you may find the services of an expert invaluable, it's important to start developing your own taste and style, and also start picking up knowledge, as soon as you can.

Although some of the very rich are often caricatured as having appalling taste, many of them, both in the United States and in Europe, have impeccable taste—like former ambassador to Denmark and the Philippines William McCormick Blair, Jr., and his wife, Deeda. Although Mrs. Blair has employed the famous decorator Billy Baldwin, she has her own ideas on decorating and her home in Washington reflects her penchant for Chinese silk scroll paintings, coromandel screens, plants, flowers and fine French furniture. Her knowledge of the subject is extensive and she prefers to live without a piece she particularly wants until she finds the perfect specimen.

The Schlumbergers—Sao and Pierre—are also great collectors. They have filled their exquisitely modernized Louis XVI house on Paris's Left Bank with Ming porcelains, signed French furnishings, and paintings and sculpture by artists like Mark Rothko ($125,000), Jackson Pollock ($150,000), Henri Matisse ($250,000), Picasso and Bonnard ($350,000). If you assume that the paintings are worth, conservatively, around $875,000, it'll give you some idea of how much all this luxury costs, though Pierre Schlumberger's extensive holdings in oil and drilling patents cover it without too much difficulty. While even the most creative financial adviser could hardly claim that the Schlumbergers' basement discotheque—walls, floor and ceiling carpeted in blue, with a stage lit from below—is an investment, practically everything else in the house is.

As Max Adler, whose collection of K'ang Hsi and Ch'ien Lung porcelain, Waterford chandeliers, Ming rugs and superb eighteenth-century American and English furniture is worth around $1.5 million, said in 1973, it's "more enjoyable than looking at stock certificates. With antiques appreciating at better than 20 percent a year, I might sell it all in 1976 for $3 million." Chances are, though, that the Alders won't sell.

Amidst these extremely gifted amateurs is Henry P. McIlhenny, for thirty years the curator of the Philadelphia Museum of Art, who has put together a private collection of paintings and furniture that any museum would be only too happy to have. It includes superb Charles X furniture as well as Chippendale, Queen Anne and Chinese

(pieces signed by Boulle and Roetgen), also paint-
ings by such varied artists as David, Ingres,
Renoir, Roualt, Toulouse-Lautrec, Corot, Van
Gogh, Dali and Warhol.

From the collectors' point of view, Mr. Mc-
Ilhenny believes, times have changed and not for
the better. "I can hardly buy a print now for what
my Ingres cost years ago. It has taken all the fun
out of it. . . . I don't like it because so many of
the people who really like works of art can't afford
to have them, whereas others buy because they
are vying for prestige."

THE COST OF THE VACATION HOUSE

Let's look at how much it costs to own a typical
vacation house. It could be in almost any area of
the country—but remember, costs are higher on
the East Coast or West Coast than, say, in the
Midwest. The expenses of a typical vacation house
would look like this:

Initial Cost:

House Cost: $150,000, mortgage at about
                $72,000, 25 years, at 7½ percent.

Furnishings: $50,000 including small boat, extra
                car, lawn equipment and new ap-
                pliances.

Repairs: $25,000, including new tennis
                court, or swimming pool, and the
                sundry expenses that you never
                think of but have to be made.

Operating Costs: One Year

Mortgages:	Principal	$1,470	
	Interest	5,209	
			$ 6,680
Insurance:	Homeowners Policy	890	
	Boat Insurance	35	
			925
Upkeep:	Fuel, Electric, Water, Telephone, Refuse Collection		1,500
	Tennis Court		650
	Repairs		300
	Daily Help (by the hour)		1,380
	Boat Tax		64
	Lawn Maintenance		650
Taxes:	Real Estate		2,000
	Fire District		179
	Sewer		166
			$14,494
	Less Mortgage Principal		1,470
			$13,024

By the time you add minimum transportation, a few parties and the many, many extras you are bound to encounter, there is no way you can get away with less than $15,000 a year. If you feel that you are saving the principal paid on the mortgage as an investment, remember that you are losing the interest that you could get on the cash invested on top of the mortgage.

The argument is always, "But the house will increase in value to compensate for this." Maybe yes, maybe no. It depends on several factors: Did you buy at the top of the market, or the bottom? Is the house the best buy in the neighborhood, or the worst, at the price to be paid? From the investment point of view, you should also remember that vacation houses are a luxury item and generally, in times of recession, the luxury market is the hardest hit, which means no buyers in times of a bad recession.

Our own experience has been mixed. Some of the people we know who have invested in vacation homes have found that this was generally their best investment; but here the comparison was usually against bad stockmarket advice rather than fixed-interest investments, and on the whole these were people who bought at least four or five years ago. Take the south of France. Unless you bought four or five years ago, you have little or no chance of coming out ahead on a house as an investment. The prices have been pushed too high because of the Italian crisis and the booming French economy.

On the other hand, from the reports we get, the Hamptons and Fire Island are booming, both sales and rentals are very good, and there are good buys around if you have the necessary cash for the down payment. The same is true of property in upstate New York, Connecticut and Massachusetts. The Caribbean is a disaster, and so is Florida. California, especially the shore areas, reports that business is very good, with bigger houses selling quite well. It could be that many areas are reporting good business because many people who used to vacation in Europe or the Caribbean are now staying home and either buying or renting a house for the summer.

Our advice: Avoid buying if you can, and rent instead. For a maximum of $10,000 a year, and probably more like $5000 to $8000, you can rent a very good house for the summer at any vacation area. Since this is much less than your probable minimum maintenance costs on any house that you owned, the wisdom of this advice from an investment point of view should be easy to see. And what's more, what would have been the cash deposit for a house, invested well in fixed-interest securities, should give you more than enough to rent and leave you a little extra holiday spending money besides.

This way, you keep that important element of flexibility, too; you can go somewhere else if you get tired of the scene, as you almost inevitably will after a couple of years.

Buying a house in order to rent it out doesn't make much sense, as you can see from the figures, unless you get a very good buy or build the house yourself. Most vacationers will want the house at the height of the season, when you most probably want to use it for yourself. More important, this again is a business to be avoided unless you are very good at it. Most people who make out on rentals are those who bought the houses many years ago, have spent little to fix them up, or just have so much money it doesn't make any difference. But we think you will find, on balance, that most of them would rather be sellers than renters, but just can't move the house. It's tough on them, but ideal for you, if you can cope with the ego problem of not owning your own vacation home.

With vacation houses, as with china, sweaters, fruit, even automobiles, beware of the "bargain." Two cautionary tales:

Arlene and Mickey Dubin, friends of ours, were looking for a small place in the country and something interesting to do. Their ideal was something not too expensive that they could also run as a small inn and restaurant. They found just what they wanted—a place in Salisbury, Connecticut, for $85,000, which had already been run as an inexpensive inn for holiday families.

Like so many country "bargains," it was in need of repair and restoration, and since the Dubins have excellent taste—Arlene used to be a buyer for Saks Fifth Avenue—and they had a very clear idea of how they wanted the place to look, they spent a further $75,000, partly through loans from banks and friends.

"The Iron Dube" opened early in 1972 and at first it did well; the area had been in need of a nice restaurant and it was attracting people from over fifty miles away. But then came 1973, the oil crisis, the general recession it brought with it, the falling stock market and the rising cost of everything from food to gas. People no longer had the gas to drive fifty miles for dinner, and even if they had, the number who could afford $40 for dinner for two sharply declined.

By the end of 1973 the only business they were doing was a small dinner crowd on a Saturday night and the occasional drinkers in the bar. Nearby Lime Rock Race Track failed to pull in substantial numbers of weekend visitors, and most of the local residents were either fixed-income coupon clippers—one of the hardest-hit groups of all—or middle-class working people who couldn't afford more than the occasional celebration dinner at the Iron Dube.

To cut costs, the Dubins reduced the staff and took over those duties themselves, but by the late fall of 1973, they packed their bags and headed for Florida.

The inn was eventually sold—but not at a profit.

Back in the early 1970s, Tony and Ethne Rudd were looking for a country cottage. Then, in Wiltshire, one of the most beautiful counties in England, they came across Chalcot House, a seventeenth-century ruin with a superb Inigo Jones facade and a not-so-superb twenty-five-bedroom Victorian extension, for a mere $24,000. The basic reconstruction of the main part of the house, and the demolition of the Victorian wing, cost them a further $100,000, leaving them with a potentially stunning nine-bedroom house in nine rolling acres of Wiltshire. It had cost them $124,000, but at 1972 prices it still looked like a bargain.

By 1973, what with the oil crisis, a fall in the stock market and rising costs, the Rudds hit trouble. The house was far from complete and their mortgage, in the cold light of "tight money" and rising interest rates, began to be a bit of a millstone. It didn't seem feasible to sell the house in its uncompleted state, so the Rudds finished the restoration and turned it into a small hotel.

So, now, Chalcot House is restored to its former glory—and former function—as a weekend retreat. The family arrives from town and prepares for the guests. The house party arrives for a weekend of games, excursions to Bath, the theater, galleries, croquet, tennis, drinks in the library, and port—passed counter-clockwise, naturally—after dinner. The only differences between the seventeenth and twentieth centuries is that some of the accents echoing round the parkland are transatlantic, and apart from the Rudds and their immediate family, the guests are paying guests. According to Mrs. Rudd, they simply could not run Chalcot House without guests, and they can't sell it except at an enormous financial loss.

Another "bargain" country home has turned out to be not such a bargain after all.

INVESTING IN PROPERTY—DON'T, UNLESS YOU KNOW WHAT YOU ARE DOING

Investments in land and buildings are specialized matters requiring specialized advice. If you are interested in land, here are some things to keep in mind.

Land without a specific use is money without a market, except for out-and-out speculators. This is a very shaky kind of investment, especially if you buy it subject to a purchase-money mortgage, or unless you are able to get a mortgage from a savings bank, which is very unlikely. The payments, which include taxes and mortgage payments, can become such a burden that unless you can turn the land quickly you had better avoid this as an investment.

A few people we know have made money in raw land in vacation areas, like the Hamptons on Long Island, New York, but they were professionals in what, again, is a strictly professional market. If you know the scene, fine. If not, find a partner who does, or stay out of the game.

Buying more than you need to build your own house, with the idea of selling off the excess to make a profit, also rarely works out unless you are lucky or unless you have enough capital to wait it out. In the long run you will probably come out ahead, but scarcely more than if you'd left the money in a savings bank.

Investing in land in faraway places, almost always with strange-sounding names, is financial suicide. These are just promotions to be avoided.

At one time or another, we are all tempted to get into land because of that long-held theory that you never go wrong with land. But don't you believe it! It's just another commodity, and as with all commodities, unless you are an expert you'll probably be the last to know when the market turns down. At least with other commodities, like paintings and furniture, you can enjoy them. A tent on a piece of land in the Caribbean is certainly not our style; it shouldn't be yours, either.

Land to build on is a different story. That's not an investment but a very big liability. Of course, like much of the advice in this book, that's only our opinion—though an informed one, we hope. Many people will disagree with us—Sylvia Porter, for one. In her *Money Book* she says that "of all millionaires, 90 percent became so through owning real estate," and "more money has been made in real estate than in all industrial investments combined."

We just don't believe it. Maybe years ago, when the opportunities were different and prices much lower, real estate—land and property—was a good investment, but not today. Prices and returns are not commensurate with the market risk. Property markets have plummeted in just the last two years, and from our point of view, as investments they are too cyclical. We would rather go for stability and good, guaranteed yields. While it is true that the value of raw land in the United States has risen greatly in the last twenty-five years, the potential gain on this kind of investment does not compensate for the cost of carrying the land, the loss of interest on your money during the period and the possibility of illiquidity.

What people tend to forget is that there is a top price for everything—be it product or real estate—beyond which it becomes uneconomical for anybody to go. Look at your own position. How high can you go for an apartment or office space? There comes a point where you must stay where you are, and this affects marketability.

Many people we know used to participate in real-estate syndications of all types—land, investment property, from apartments to office buildings—and we are sure that but for the tax advantage most of them would have been better off in other investments that offered the same kinds of shelters. Many people we know lost their principal, as well as any yield, because this market, again, is best left to the expert. What you must guard against is all of those people—friends, neighbors and associates—who tell you that they have made big profits in land, building developments, vacation resorts, shopping centers, industrial plant sites and so on. The truth is that many of them have actually lost their shirts, but are too embarrassed to tell you the truth.

In short, this is one of the most overrated investment areas there is, because of the costs involved and the investment's lack of liquidity. Also, in all parts of the country, property taxes— a major part of the cost of owning property—have soared, and it looks to us as though they'll be going even higher before they come down.

Many people were so accustomed to low interest rates on mortgages that they forgot what it means to have to refinance the mortgage at 14 percent interest instead of 6 percent—not only to their own income, but also to any potential buyer of their house, who may even find it impossible to get a mortgage at all. And while real estate was supposed to be an inflation hedge in a prolonged business recession, the property market was the first to fall and its liquidity ceased to exist at all.

Unlike stocks or fixed-interest securities, there is really no formal market at all for the buying or selling of real estate. If you want to be in that market, you are better off being the lender, the mortgagor, than the owner. When we had a house to sell and couldn't find a buyer because it was impossible for anyone to get a mortgage, we decided to act as bankers ourselves, offering the house at a fair price with financing in the form of a purchase-money mortgage at 10 percent over five years. Now, with the prime interest rate down to 8 percent, we have a good 10-percent fixed-interest security, and the house, we know, represents good collateral.

If you're interested, the key here is to get enough of a down payment so that if the buyer walks away from his obligation you can resell the house at a reasonable price. You must also be especially careful of your purchaser, because if he is not likely to care for the house, the cost of the repairs he leaves you to do may offset his down payment.

We subscribe to the view that you should own your principal residence, mortgaged as high as possible, and nothing else. If you need other property, rent it, don't buy it—the hidden costs will eat you alive. Even with your own principal residence, unless you can get the benefit of great leverage and borrow at least 75 percent of the purchase price, you are better off renting. With a high mortgage, you will get the benefit of the interest deductions and forced savings. Best of all, the loan is the best hedge against inflation because you will be borrowing expensive dollars and paying back in cheap dollars over the years.

Remember, unlike investment property, many of the costs of your principal residence will occur whether you buy or rent, and in the last analysis at least that real-estate investment will give you a chance to live better, to compensate for the real loss on yield.

Beware of bargains. There aren't many. Everything has its value and you get what you pay for, nothing more, nothing less. Avoid buying speculative property in the country; property that may be rezoned when you don't want it to be and may not be rezoned when you speculated that it would be; property near airports that are going to become bigger; property already in the process of unwanted change, etc., etc. From bitter experience, we know they don't work as investments. The promises are usually not fulfilled—that's why they are bargains.

Buy, if at all, for a specific purpose: to build your own house; or to sell; to fix up and resell; to resell with a purchase-money mortgage; or for the guaranteed yield from a first-class tenant. But remember, what used to be a first-class tenant in the 1960s is no longer necessarily a first-class tenant in the 1970s. Look at Interstate Department Stores, Beck Industries, W. T. Grant, who were all considered first-class credits years ago and who are all in the bankruptcy courts today.

If you buy for investment, which means yield,

then make sure you understand the real risk. Steer clear of commercial property—leave that to the professionals—and don't be deluded by the tax shelters, because a loss is a loss; all the shelter does is postpone a profit. And if you lose your principal investment, the tax shelter is meaningless.

THE COST OF OWNING A HORSE

You may be one of a growing number of sports-minded people who have thought about buying a horse—for your child to ride or just for your own pleasure, or as an investment. Be forewarned that the pleasures of ownership come at a stiff price—especially in feeding and caring for the horse.

Figure on an initial $500 to $1500 to buy the animal and another $500 to $2000 for riding equipment. Beyond that, the annual cost of keeping a horse can run from $900 to $2500.

If you're still interested at those prices, a local riding stable is probably the best place to buy your first horse; or, if they haven't anything suitable, they could recommend someone with a horse to sell. Any agricultural school or the county agent in your area can provide free information about horses, and some keep tabs on reliable breeders. They should also be able to recommend a good veterinarian and a farrier, a blacksmith who works only with horses. Both should examine any horse you're interested in before you buy—which will cost you $20 to $30. You should also ask their advice about whether the horse fits the rider's needs and, more important, level of horsemanship.

Once the animal is yours, the annual bill for shots, deworming and teeth filings will run you at least $60 to $150. The farrier bill is steeper— $150 to $250 per year—since horseshoes must be changed every five to eight weeks and cost $12 to $25 for four. If you can keep the horse on your own property, figure on $40 to $80 per month for hay and feed. The alternative is to board your horse at a stable, where monthly fees range from $75 to $150 and usually include feed, hay, watering, and straw for the floor.

But the biggest financial shock occurs at the tack shop, where you buy riding equipment and apparel. You'll spend $500 to $2000 just for the bare necessities—including $100 to $1000 for a saddle; $15 to $150 for bridle, bit and reins; and $28 to $70 for stirrups, cinch and girth. No wonder the Indians rode bareback!

Clothing doesn't *have* to be expensive. You can ride in jeans and heavy-duty shoes or boots, though a hard hat and a pair of riding boots are mandatory for jumping your horse, and they'll cost $100 to $250. Should you or your child enter riding competitions, apparel costs really pile up. Proper attire, from breeches to riding jackets, can run $200 to $350.

Prestige comes expensive.

8

CONCLUSION, IF ANY

Living rich, as you'll have no doubt realized by now, takes a lot of energy, thought and careful planning, and if you are going to do it successfully, then perhaps the most important lesson to learn is to control your spending, and not let it control you.

If you have no major financial problems, you may assume that you are in control of your spending. Most people do make that assumption and it's only when they find themselves in real trouble financially that they realize, too late, that their assumption was wrong.

The cause of the trouble is rarely one major extravagance; it is usually the cumulative effect of a "little extra" on everything, and the spending spiral is such an attractive and easy one to get into that you seldom notice that it's happening.

As you move up the income ladder, you naturally want to improve your life-style, especially as you can now afford to. So you buy a second car—you need one to drive to work and avoid all the hassels of public transportation, and your wife needs one for the shopping and to ferry the kids around. A perfectly justifiable extra expense—on the surface, anyway.

The same is true of clothes. A man in your position is expected to dress accordingly, so you shop at better stores, and maybe buy a tailor-made suit or jacket for the special occasion.

And how can you not justify two or three vacations, when everyone around you is doing the same? The sun in the winter, or the ski slopes at some northern resort, and of course the traditional summer vacation—haven't you *earned* them? And how can your kids not go to camp when all their friends are going?

If you live in the city, then naturally you'll want them to go to private schools, too. Eventually there is the second home, longer and more exotic vacations, jewelry and furs for your wife to wear on special occasions. (In India a man's wealth is judged by his wife's plumpness; in America it's judged by the number of karats he puts on her fingers.)

It all starts to creep up on you so gradually that you never actually realize that you've been living beyond your means since way back. It's something you don't want to think about, and certainly nothing to discuss with your wife because merely discussing it implies a sense of failure, and, after all, aren't you a success at what you have done? Many of your neighbors, friends, and relatives seem to be living as well as you are, if not better. How do they manage it? Are they more successful than you are?

No, it's a subject that does not bear too close a scrutiny and which, you figure, will work itself out. It did last year, and the year before.

You may think that because we've been talking in terms of spending hundreds of thousands of dollars each year, figures that are way above your level, that the message does not apply to you. Wrong! It is not the amounts that lead to financial success or failure, it's the percentages.

If your income is $10,000 and your spending is $11,000, you are in just as much trouble as you would be if your income were $100,000 and your spending $110,000. You might dismiss a woman spending $25,000 a year on clothing as absurd, but spending $2500, or even $250, is just as absurd if it represents the same percentage of your income.

As you'll have gathered by now, however, most people do live beyond their means, no matter how high their income, so the important thing to learn, no matter what your income, is how to do it successfully!

Before you can hope to come up with any answers, you must first understand the nature of the problem. It is never merely a question of saving a few dollars here or a few dollars there— three weeks on Cap-Ferrat instead of four, a 1961 Romanée Conti instead of a 1953. What it requires is a fundamental examination of the way you live and what your real priorities are.

Four years ago we sat down and did just that. We decided that we did not *need* the big house in New York, or the house in California, or the Lear jet, so we sold them. We decided that the lavish vacations we had been taking were not actually necessary for our happiness, so we started taking fewer of them, and in a more economical fashion, and so on.

The key to success is learning to control both your spending *and* your saving—the two go hand in hand and can only work successfully together. The first step is drawing up a budget, listing your income and *everything* you spend. We recommend that you do it sitting down because it's likely to give you quite a nasty shock, but it is essential if you are ever going to live rich successfully.

The second step is to look very carefully at the

people you know or only read about in the papers who seem to be living much better than you are. Are they really richer than you, or are they, like some of those mentioned in this book, living rich extremely successfully off the corporation? At the risk of repeating ourselves, it's probably the best way there is to live rich, so why not investigate its potential for you? If you find that it isn't an avenue open to you, then at least knowing that it's the means by which people manage to live rich may give you some peace of mind.

Don't forget, either, that some people spend out of insecurity—they believe not that you are what you eat, but that you are what you spend, and thus have a psychological need to "keep up appearances."

Then again, take the Howard Bellins. While we wouldn't advocate their life-style—lock, stock and barrel—they certainly offer a valuable object lesson in how, if you *are* secure and full of self-confidence, you can jet-set at half-price.

And do not overlook that honorable old profession of freeloading! Why shouldn't you have your share of the freebies available in this world? Maybe you're too proud, or maybe you just never considered that it was a possibility.

If you are going to spend some of your own money, then think very carefully about what you're doing. Does your wife *really* need to spend that much on clothes? Getting onto the Best Dressed List does not automatically mean that you become a worthwhile, interesting person. Perhaps it might be better to cut down on Gucci handbags and invest a little in a college course on world politics or the modern American novel.

And do you really need that vacation house?

Can you afford not just to buy it but to run it? What about the costs of getting there, and paying someone to look after it during the fifty weeks a year you aren't there? And will you be able to sell it without taking a loss when you are tired of it?

When you take a hard look at the way some of the rich spend their money—$100,000 parties for 500 people, of whom perhaps 50 are real friends, 200 merely acquaintances and the rest practitioners of the fine art of living rich at no cost—it does all seem a little senseless, doesn't it?

But, as we said earlier, controlling your spending is only one side of the street. The other is learning how to make your investments work for you.

A lot of people have just as many problems with their low-yielding investments as they have with their spending habits. A while back, we got a letter from the president of a small university who is having problems with his university's spending. We wrote back suggesting some of the things recommended in this book as a means of improving the investment yield of his endowment fund. Just the other day we heard from him again.

"First," he wrote, "your observation concerning a relatively low return on our endowment is correct. I'm frustrated by seeing private entrepreneurs developing a much higher return on their capital than we do with our endowment. When I challenge this, I constantly get the answer of, 'Well, that's the way it's done in higher education.'"

Therein lies the key to learning how to live rich. It does *not* have to be done that way if you are prepared to take the time, energy and effort to learn an alternative way. A lot of individuals fall into the same category, only they say, "I'm too busy running my business to learn how to invest my money."

Maybe they would not have to work so hard to live rich if they took the time and trouble to understand the proper way to invest their money for a better yield. Spending goes hand in glove with investing, whether at a university or in your own household. The businessman knows that increasing sales is easier than cutting expenses, but once he leaves the office he forgets that the same rules apply to his home as to his business.

What *Living Rich* set out to do was not to give you all the answers (though quite a few people have lived rich for years on claims that they could!) but to make you aware of all the possibilities open to you, so that, having examined them, you can decide which are the most attractive to you.

In the end, however, if you'll pardon the cliché, it's worth pointing out that money cannot buy happiness—ultimately an unhappy marriage or an empty existence cannot be cured by spending —though as a comedian once said, if you're rich you can at least be miserable in comfort!

THE BEST BUSINESS GUIDES AVAILABLE TODAY FROM PLAYBOY PAPERBACKS

MICHAEL DOYLE &
DAVID STRAUS
__16614 **HOW TO MAKE** $2.50
        MEETINGS WORK

AUREN URIS
__16616 **MASTERY OF MANAGEMENT** $2.25

JEFFREY FEINMAN
__16797 **100 SUREFIRE BUSINESSES** $2.50
        YOU CAN START WITH
        LITTLE OR NO INVESTMENT

MAX GUNTHER
__16645 **THE VERY, VERY RICH AND** $2.50
        HOW THEY GOT THAT WAY

NICOLAS DARVAS
__16465 **YOU CAN STILL MAKE IT** $1.95
        IN THE STOCK MARKET

MICHAEL LAURENCE
__16643 **PLAYBOY'S INVESTMENT** $2.50
        GUIDE